LAWS AND LEGISLATION

FEDERAL GOVERNMENT AND THE REINS ACT

MAJOR REGULATIONS

Laws and Legislation

Additional books in this series can be found on Nova's website under the Series tab.

Additional E-books in this series can be found on Nova's website under the E-book tab.

LAWS AND LEGISLATION

FEDERAL GOVERNMENT AND THE REINS ACT

MAJOR REGULATIONS

LISA MATTHEWS
AND
JASON FANNING
EDITORS

Nova Science Publishers, Inc.
New York

For permission to use material from this book please contact us:
Telephone 631-231-7269; Fax 631-231-8175
Web Site: http://www.novapublishers.com

NOTICE TO THE READER

Additional color graphics may be available in the e-book version of this book.

LIBRARY OF CONGRESS CATALOGING-IN-PUBLICATION DATA

Federal government and the REINS Act : major regulations / Editors: Lisa Matthews and Jason Fanning.
p. cm.
Includes index.
ISBN 978-1-62100-346-5 (hardcover)
1. Delegated legislation--United States. 2. Legislative oversight--United States. 3. Administrative acts--United States. 4. United States. Congress--Powers and duties. I. Fanning, Jason. II. Matthews, Lisa (Lisa A.), 1941.
KF4583.F43 2012
348.73'25--dc23

2011032637

Published by Nova Science Publishers, Inc. † New York

CONTENTS

PREFACE

Under the Congressional Review Act, a covered agency regulation takes effect as provided by law unless Congress disapproves the rule with a joint resolution of disapproval. In contrast, the Regulations from the Executive In Need of Security (REINS) Act would generally require the enactment of a joint resolution of approval before any "major rule" could take effect. This book provides information on the types of "major rules" that may be covered by the REINS Act, if enacted. Specifically, it identifies how many major rules have been issued in recent years, and which agencies have issued them along with identifying why certain rules published during calendar year 2010 were considered to be major rules under the CRA.

Chapter 1 - Under the Congressional Review Act (CRA, 5 U.S.C. §§ 801-808), a covered agency regulation takes effect as provided by law unless Congress disapproves the rule with a joint resolution of disapproval. In contrast, the Regulations from the Executive In Need of Scrutiny (REINS) Act (H.R. 10 and S. 299, 112th Congress) would (if enacted) generally require the enactment of a joint resolution of *approval* before any "*major rule*" could take effect (e.g., rules that are expected to have a $100 million annual impact on the economy). This report provides information on the types of "major rules" that may be covered by the REINS Act, if enacted. Specifically, it identifies how many major rules have been issued in recent years, and which agencies have issued them. It also attempts to identify why certain rules published during calendar year 2010 were considered to be major rules under the CRA.

Chapter 2 - Chairman Coble and Ranking Member Cohen and Members of the Subcommittee, thank you for the opportunity to appear before you today. The author is appearing in his own capacity and not representing any other person. The hearing raises some of the most important issues facing the nation today: Does our current regulatory system undermine economic recovery and hold the private sector back from creating new jobs? And, how can we reform the regulatory process to provide more accountability and encourage better regulations that reduce their costs, thereby unleashing economic growth and the creation of more jobs?

Chapter 3 - Over the past several decades, the scope, reach and cost of federal regulations have increased dramatically. From the 1950s through the 2000s, the amount of federal regulatory activity, as measured by pages in the *Federal Register*, has increased more than six-fold. In the 1950s, federal agencies published an average of just under 11,000 pages in the *Federal Register* per year. From 2001-2009, federal agencies averaged over 73,000 pages per year. In 2010, the *Federal Register* contained over 82,000 pages, the greatest number in over a decade and the third highest total in our nation's history. The number of new final rules each year has declined, but federal regulations are still adopted at a rapid pace. In 2008 and 2009 federal regulatory agencies adopted 3,830 and 3,503 final rules, respectively. These rules cover everything from greenhouse gas emission reporting and proxy disclosures to electronic fund transfers and the energy and water use of home appliances. Substantially more regulation is on the way. By some estimates, the Wall Street Reform and Consumer Protection Act alone will require over 200 federal rulemakings.

Chapter 4 – The author served as the Administrator of the Office of Information and Regulatory Affairs (OIRA) at the Office of Management and Budget (OMB) for the first five years of the Clinton Administration, then as the Deputy Assistant to the President for Economic Policy and Deputy Director of the National Economic Council, and then as the Deputy Director for Management of OMB. After leaving government service in January 2001, she taught administrative law courses at the University of Michigan Law School, George Washington University Law School, George Mason University Law School, and the University of Pennsylvania Law School, and she also taught American Government courses to undergraduates at Smith College, Johns Hopkins University, and the University of Michigan in Washington Program; this semester, the author is teaching a seminar in advanced administrative law at NYU Law School and is a Senior Adviser at the Podesta Group. Before entering government service, the author was the Chair of the ABA Section on Administrative Law and Regulatory Practice (1988-89), and during her government service, she was the Vice Chair (and Acting Chair) of the Administrative Conference of the United States (ACUS). The author has written articles for scholarly publications and has frequently been asked to speak on administrative law in general and rulemaking in particular.

In: Federal Government and the REINS Act ISBN: 978-1-62100-346-5
Editors: L. Matthews and J. Fanning

Chapter 1

REINS ACT: NUMBER AND TYPES OF "MAJOR RULES" IN RECENT YEARS*

Curtis W. Copeland and Maeve P. Carey

SUMMARY

Under the Congressional Review Act (CRA, 5 U.S.C. §§ 801-808), a covered agency regulation takes effect as provided by law unless Congress disapproves the rule with a joint resolution of disapproval. In contrast, the Regulations from the Executive In Need of Scrutiny (REINS) Act (H.R. 10 and S. 299, 112th Congress) would (if enacted) generally require the enactment of a joint resolution of *approval* before any "*major rule*" could take effect (e.g., rules that are expected to have a $100 million annual impact on the economy). This report provides information on the types of "major rules" that may be covered by the REINS Act, if enacted. Specifically, it identifies how many major rules have been issued in recent years, and which agencies have issued them. It also attempts to identify why certain rules published during calendar year 2010 were considered to be major rules under the CRA.

According to a database maintained by the Government Accountability Office (GAO), in 9 of the 14 full calendar years since the CRA was enacted, federal agencies published between 50 and 70 major rules. The agencies published 76 major rules in 1998, and 77 major rules

* This is an edited, reformatted and augmented version of a Congressional Research Service publication, CRS Report for Congress R41651, from www.crs.gov, dated on February 24, 2011.

in 2000. The number of major rules issued in a single calendar year first exceeded 80 in 2008 (the last full year of the George W. Bush Administration), when 95 major rules were published. In calendar year 2009, the first year of the Barack Obama Administration, federal agencies published 84 major final rules. However, 11 of those 84 rules were actually issued in early January 2009, during the final days of the Bush Administration. During calendar year 2010, federal agencies published 100 major final rules. The entities that issued the largest number of major rules from 2004 through 2010 were the Departments of Health and Human Services, Agriculture, and the Interior, and the Environmental Protection Agency.

CRS examined the 100 major rules published in 2010 and concluded that they appeared to be "major" for a variety of reasons. Thirty-seven of the rules appeared to be major because they involved transfers of funds from one party to another party, most commonly the transfer of federal funds to the recipients of those funds (e.g., grants, food stamps, Medicare or Medicaid funds, special pay for members of the military, and crop payments). Ten other rules appeared to be major because they were expected to prompt consumer spending, or because they were establishing fees for the reimbursement of particular federal functions (e.g., issuance of passports and oversight of the nuclear power industry). Thirty-nine rules appeared to be major because they were expected to result in at least \$100 million in annual compliance costs, regulatory benefits, or both. In 20 of those 39 rules, estimated costs and benefits were both expected to exceed \$100 million. In 14 of these rules, the agencies' lowest estimates of regulatory benefits were larger than the highest estimated compliance costs. In only one rule were the lowest costs greater than the highest benefits, and the agency indicated that this result was caused by the lack of discretion provided in the underlying statute. These variations in the type of major rules do not bring into question the appropriateness of congressional oversight. However, Congress may need different types of expertise to oversee different types of major rules. H.R. 214 (112th Congress), which would create a Congressional Office of Regulatory Analysis, may provide access to that expertise.

INTRODUCTION

The Congressional Review Act (CRA, 5 U.S.C. §§ 801-808) requires each federal agency to send its covered final rules to the Comptroller General at the Government Accountability Office (GAO) and to both houses of Congress before the rules can take effect.[1] The CRA generally requires agencies to delay the effective dates of "major" final rules until 60 days after the date that the rules are published in the *Federal Register* or submitted to Congress, whichever is later.[2]

The act also requires the Comptroller General to provide a report to the congressional committees of jurisdiction within 15 calendar days after each major rule is submitted or published, with the report summarizing the issuing agency's compliance with relevant rulemaking requirements.[3] The CRA defines a "major rule" as

> any rule that the Administrator of the Office of Information and Regulatory Affairs [OIRA] of the Office of Management and Budget [OMB] finds has resulted in or is likely to result in—(A) an annual effect on the economy of $100,000,000 or more; (B) a major increase in costs or prices for consumers, individual industries, Federal, State, or local government agencies, or geographic regions; or (C) significant adverse effects on competition, employment, investment, productivity, innovation, or on the ability of United States-based enterprises to compete with foreign-based enterprises in domestic and export markets. The term does not include any rule promulgated under the Telecommunications Act of 1996 and the amendments made by that Act.[4]

The CRA also established expedited legislative procedures (primarily in the Senate) by which Congress may disapprove any final rule (not just major rules) by enacting a joint resolution of disapproval (which requires subsequent signature by the President). Signed into law on March 29, 1996, as part of the Small Business Regulatory Enforcement Fairness Act (SBREFA, Title II of P.L. 104-121, 5 U.S.C. § 601 note), the CRA was an attempt to reestablish a measure of congressional authority over rulemaking. However, in the nearly 15 years since the CRA's enactment, it has been used to disapprove one rule.[5]

REINS Act

Under the CRA, an agency regulation takes effect as provided by law unless Congress disapproves the rule with a CRA joint resolution of disapproval.[6] In contrast, the Regulations from the Executive In Need of Scrutiny (REINS) Act (H.R. 10 and S. 299, 112th Congress) would (if enacted) generally require the enactment of a joint resolution of *approval* before any "major rule" could take effect.[7] Specifically, the REINS Act would amend Chapter 8 of Title 5, United States Code, and in the new Section 802, would require that a joint resolution of approval be introduced within three session days or legislative days after a major rule is submitted to Congress. The bills also states that if a joint resolution of approval for a major rule is not enacted by the end of 90 session days or legislative days after such resolution is introduced, the rule shall be deemed not to be approved and shall not take effect. However, according to the new Section 801 of Title 5, a major rule could take effect for 90 calendar days without such approval if the President determines that it is necessary because of an imminent threat to health or safety or other emergency, for the enforcement of criminal laws, for national security, or to implement an international trade agreement.

The REINS Act states that its purpose is "to increase accountability for and transparency in the federal regulatory process." It goes on to say that

> Section 1 of article I of the United States Constitution grants all legislative powers to Congress. Over time, Congress has excessively delegated its constitutional charge while failing to conduct appropriate oversight and retain accountability for the content of the laws it passes. By requiring a vote in Congress, the REINS Act will result in more carefully drafted and detailed legislation, an improved regulatory process, and a legislative branch that is truly accountable to the American people for the laws imposed upon them.[8]

Comments Regarding the REINS Act

Reactions to the REINS Act from non-governmental observers have been mixed. Several of these observers have expressed support for the act. For example, an editorial in the *Wall Street Journal* stated that the legislation "would revolutionize government in practice and help restore the representative democracy the founders envisioned."[9] Wayne Crews of the Competitive Enterprise Institute said major rules "are the ones costing $100 million annually," and said that "reaffirming Congress' accountability to voters for agencies' most costly rules is a basic principle of good government."[10] Phil Kerpen of Americans for Prosperity said that the REINS Act "is the most important legislative effort to reform the regulatory process in Congress."[11] At a January 24, 2011, hearing held by the House Committee on the Judiciary's Subcommittee on Courts, Commercial and Administrative Law, Jonathan H. Adler, a professor of law at Case Western Reserve University School of Law, said that the REINS Act "offers a promising mechanism for disciplining federal regulatory agencies and enhancing Congressional accountability for federal regulations."[12]

Other observers, however, have expressed concerns about the legislation. For example, Sidney Shapiro of the Center for Progressive Reform said,

> The REINS Act would make Congress the final arbiter of all significant regulatory decisions. While superficially this may seem like a good idea – after all, Members of Congress are elected and regulators are not – the REINS Act would replace what is good about agency rulemaking with what is bad about the legislative process. Neither Members of Congress nor their staffs are likely to have sufficient scientific, engineering and economic expertise regarding complex regulations. And, unlike agencies, Congress does not have to have good policy reasons for refusing to approve a regulation. Instead, the approval process is likely to be nakedly political, reflecting the raw political power of special interests and the large campaign donations that they give.[13]

Concerns have also been raised regarding the constitutionality of the congressional approval process contemplated by the REINS Act, and the amount of time that it would take to approve all major rules each year. For example, at the above-mentioned January 24, 2011, hearing on the REINS Act, Sally Katzen, a professor of law and former Administrator of OIRA, raised several constitutional issues regarding the proposed legislation. Overall, she said that the REINS Act "is not well considered, it is not tailored to the problem it is attempting to solve, and it will inevitably have unintended but nonetheless significant adverse effects on the economy and society at large, including fundamentally changing our constitutional form of government."[14]

Methodology Used in this Report

This report provides information on the types of "major rules" that may be subject to the REINS Act, if it is enacted. Specifically, the report identifies how many major rules have been issued in recent years, and which agencies have issued them. It also attempts to identify why OIRA considered certain rules published during calendar year 2010 to be major rules under the CRA. The Appendix to this report provides a chronological list of the major rules from 2010, along with information that GAO and the agencies provided on the economic effects of the rules.

To determine the number of major rules that have been issued and which agencies issued them, CRS used the GAO database of rules submitted to the Comptroller General pursuant to the requirement in the CRA. That database (available at http://www.gao.gov/fedrules/) allows users to identify the number of rules that were published in the *Federal Register* by year and by cabinet department and within an "Independent Agencies and Government

Corporations" category, and to determine which of the rules were considered "major rules." CRS considers the GAO database to be one of the most authoritative and accessible sources of information regarding final rules and major final rules pursuant to the CRA.

Because the CRA states that the OIRA Administrator is to determine which rules are to be considered "major," CRS initially contacted OIRA and OMB officials, and asked for their assistance in determining why certain rules published during calendar year 2010 were classified as "major rules."[15] Although OIRA did not discuss exactly why particular rules were considered major, the current associate administrator of OIRA did provide information regarding the criteria that OIRA uses to make those determinations. For example, he said that OIRA considers a rule "major" if any related economic effects (e.g., compliance costs, regulatory benefits, federal budgetary transfers, fees, or consumer spending) are expected to meet or exceed the $100 million threshold in any year.[16]

The previously mentioned GAO database provides links to GAO's major rule reports that summarize agencies' compliance with certain rulemaking requirements. One section of those reports summarizes the agencies' cost-benefit analyses, to the extent that the agencies prepared such analyses. CRS used that information to analyze why the major rules appeared to be considered "major" under the CRA. When the information in the GAO reports did not clearly indicate the reason (e.g., because the agency did not prepare a cost-benefit analysis, or when the summary did not provide estimates of economic effects), CRS reviewed the preambles to the rules to determine why the rules appeared to be considered major.[17] The conclusions that CRS reached were based on the best available information, and were arrived at using the same general criteria that OIRA reportedly uses to make those determinations. Nevertheless, the conclusions are only our informed assessments. For that reason, this report states that certain rules "appeared" to be major for certain reasons.

Number of Major Rules and the Agencies that Issued Them

The previously mentioned *Wall Street Journal* editorial stated that the number of major rules issued by federal agencies had increased substantially during the Barack Obama Administration, from an average of between 30 and

40 rules per year during the previous 25 years to 59 in 2009 and 62 in 2010.[18] Susan Dudley, director of the George Washington University Regulatory Policy Center and former Administrator of OIRA, wrote that the Obama Administration had issued an average of 66 major rules per year during its first two years in office, compared to 47 and 48 major rules per year during the Clinton Administration and the Bush Administration, respectively.[19] Other observers have offered different counts for the number of major rules issued in recent years.[20]

CRS is not aware of any data on the number of major final rules published prior to March 1996, when the CRA was enacted.[21] As Table 1 below indicates, however, GAO's database of rules submitted to the Comptroller General shows that in 9 of the 14 full calendar years since the CRA was enacted, federal agencies published between 50 and 70 major rules. The agencies issued 76 major rules in 1998 and 77 major rules in 2000. The number of major rules issued during a single calendar year first exceeded 80 in 2008 (the last full year of the George W. Bush Administration), when 95 major rules were published. In calendar year 2009, the first calendar year of the Obama Administration, federal agencies issued 84 major final rules. However, 11 of those 84 rules were actually issued in early January 2009, during final days of the Bush Administration.[22] During calendar year 2010, federal agencies published 100 major final rules.

Another way to discuss the GAO data on major rules is by comparing time periods during recent administrations. The results vary depending on which time periods are chosen. For example, see the following:

- During the last full year of the Bush Administration (from January 22, 2008, through January 21, 2009), federal agencies published 102 major rules. During the first full year of the Obama Administration (from January 22, 2009, through January 21, 2010), federal agencies published 79 major rules.
- During the last two full years of the Bush Administration (from January 22, 2007, through January 21, 2009), federal agencies published 168 major rules. During the first two full years of the Obama Administration (from January 22, 2009, through January 21, 2011), federal agencies published 175 major rules.
- During the first full year of the Bush Administration (from January 22, 2001, through January 21, 2002), federal agencies published 54 major rules. During the first full year of the Obama Administration

(from January 22, 2009, through January 21, 2010), federal agencies published 79 major rules.

- During the first two full years of the Bush Administration (from January 22, 2001, through January 21, 2003), federal agencies published 103 major rules. During the first two full years of the Obama Administration (from January 22, 2009, through January 21, 2011), federal agencies published 175 major rules.

Table 1. Number of Final Rules and Major Final Rules by Calendar Year: 1997-2010

Calendar Year	Number of Final Rules	Number of Major Final Rules
1997	3,960	61
1998	4,420	76
1999	4,373	51
2000	4,113	77
2001	3,454	70
2002	3,608	51
2003	3,785	50
2004	3,703	66
2005	3,352	56
2006	3,083	56
2007	2,971	61
2008	3,117	95
2009	3,492	84
2010	3,271	100

Source: GAO rules database, available at http://www.gao.gov/fedrules/, as of February 15, 2011.

Table 1 also indicates that the number of major rules issued in a particular year is not strongly correlated with the number of final rules that were issued during the year. For example, in 1999, federal agencies published 4,373 final rules (the second largest number of rules during the 14 full calendar years since the enactment of the CRA), but only 51 major rules (the second lowest number of major rules during this period). The years with the largest number of major rules (2008 and 2010) were also years in which the total number of final rules issued was relatively low.

Agencies Issuing Major Rules

Table 2 below shows the number of final rules and major final rules by cabinet department and agency from 2004 through 2010. (The starting point of 2004 was selected because that was the first full year that the Department of Homeland Security was in existence, and government organization has been relatively stable since that date.) The table indicates that the number of rules and major rules issued has varied considerably by department and agency, and that the number of final rules that an agency issues is not necessarily an indication of how many major rules the agency will issue. For example, although the Department of Commerce published more than 2,000 final rules during this period, only 6 of those rules (0.2%) were considered "major." In contrast, the Department of Health and Human Services (HHS) issued 627 final rules from 2004 through 2010, of which 144 (23%) were considered major rules.

Table 2. Number of Final Rules and Major Final Rules by Department or Agency: Calendar Years 2004-2010

Department/Agency	Number of Final Rules	Number of Major Final Rules
Agriculture (USDA)	1,266	49
Commerce (DOC)	2,144	6
Defense (DOD)	662	15
Education (ED)	142	16

Table 2. (Continued)

Department/Agency	Number of Final Rules	Number of Major Final Rules
Energy (DOE)	192	17
Health and Human Services (HHS)	627	144
Homeland Security (DHS)	4,938	20
Housing and Urban Development(HUD)	151	6
Interior (DOI)	540	49
Justice (DOJ)	145	6
Labor (DOL)	180	17
State (DOS)	100	2
Treasury (TREAS)	693	8
Transportation (DOT)	5,658	31
Veterans Affairs (DVA)	157	6
Environmental Protection Agency (EPA)	3,119	40
Federal Communications	759	14
Commission (FCC)		
Federal Reserve System (FRS)	70	15
Nuclear Regulatory Commission (NRC)	126	9
Other Independent Agencies and Government Corporations	1,190	14
Total	23,003	518

Source: GAO rules database, available at http://www.gao.gov/fedrules/, as of February 15, 2011.

Note: Agencies in the "Other Independent Agencies and Government Corporations" grouping include the Federal Deposit Insurance Corporation, the General Services Administration, and the Social Security Administration. DOD rules include those that GAO reports separately for the Department of the Air Force and the Department of the Army.

RULES APPEAR TO BE "MAJOR" FOR A VARIETY OF REASONS

As noted earlier in this report, the CRA generally defines a "major rule" as one that OIRA concludes "has resulted in or is likely to result in (A) an annual effect on the economy of $100,000,000 or more; (B) a major increase in costs or prices for consumers, individual industries, Federal, State, or local government agencies, or geographic regions; or (C) significant adverse effects on competition, employment, investment, productivity, innovation, or on the ability of United States-based enterprises to compete with foreign-based enterprises in domestic and export markets." Within the first of these three definitional categories, OMB reports, agency rules, and the current OIRA associate administrator indicate that a rule may have a $100 million annual "effect on the economy" in any of several ways.[23] For example, if a rule is expected to have $100 million in compliance costs in any one year, it would likely be considered a "major" rule. If a rule is expected to produce economic benefits in any one year that are valued at $100 million, that rule would also likely be considered "major." Other rules that increase or reduce federal grants, subsidies, or other types of "transfer" payments by at least $100 million in any year, or rules that increase federal fees or other revenues by at least $100 million in a year, would also appear to meet this definition of a major rule. Also, if a rule is expected to yield a $100 million "consumer surplus" during a year by triggering consumer spending, it would also appear to be a "major rule."

Table 3 below takes the 100 major rules that were published during calendar year 2010 and, using information in GAO's reports on the major rules and information in the preambles to the rules themselves, illustrates which of the various definitions of a "major rule" appear to be applicable to them (i.e., why the rules were considered "major"). The table divides the category of "$100 million annual effect on the economy" into five subcategories (compliance costs, regulatory benefits, transfers, consumer surplus, and fees and revenues). In some cases, more than one category or subcategory applies to a single rule. For example, if a rule was expected to result in at least $100 million in annual compliance costs and was also expected to result in at least $100 million in annual benefits, then both subcategories would appear to apply. Therefore, the number of explanations provided overall (and sometimes by agency) exceeds the number of rules issued.

Table 3. Why Rules Appeared to be "Major" by Agency: Calendar Year 2010

	$100 Million Annual Effect on the Economy Due to…					
Agency (Number of Major Rules)	Regulatory Costs	Regulatory Benefits	Transfers	Consumer Surplus	Fees and Revenues	Major Increase in Costs/Prices
USDA (6)	—	—	5	—	—	1
DOD (4)	—	—	4	—	—	—
ED (5)	1	—	4	—	—	—
DOE (4)	2	3	1	—	—	—
HHS (21)	6	2	16	—	—	—
DHS (3)	—	—	1	—	2	—
HUD (1)	—	1	—	—	—	—
DOI (7)	1	1	—	6	—	—
DOJ (3)	2	3	—	—	—	—
DOL (3)	2	2	—	—	—	1
DOS (1)	—	—	—	—	1	—
DOT (4)	4	4	—	—	—	—
TREAS (3)	—	2	—	—	—	1
DVA (2)	—	—	2	—	—	—
CPSC (1)	1	—	—	—	—	—
EPA (8)	7	8	—	—	—	—
FRS (5)	—	1	—	—	—	4
NRC (1)	—	—	—	—	1	—

	$100 Million Annual Effect on the Economy Due to...					
Agency (Number of Major Rules)	Regulatory Costs	Regulatory Benefits	Transfers	Consumer Surplus	Fees and Revenues	Major Increase in Costs/Prices
SEC (9)	2	1	—	—	—	6
TREAS/ DOL/	—	—	4	—	—	3
HHS (6)						
TREAS/ FRS/	—	—	—	—	—	1
FDIC (1)						
FRS/ FTC (1)	1	—	—	—	—	—
EPA/ DOT (1)	1	1	—	—	—	—
Total (100)	30	29	37	6	4	17

Source: CRS, based on information in GAO's major rule reports and the rules themselves.

Notes: A rule may appear to be "major" for more than one reason (e.g., annual regulatory costs and benefits are each expected to exceed $100 million). Therefore, the number of rules issued by an agency may be less than the number of explanations provided. Agencies are presented first by cabinet department, then by independent agency, and finally by groups of agencies that issued certain rules. Agency abbreviations not previously identified are CPSC (Consumer Product Safety Commission), FDIC (Federal Deposit Insurance Corporation), and FTC (Federal Trade Commission).

However, if a rule appeared to be major because it had $100 million or more in annual compliance costs, CRS did not also code it as having a "major" increase in costs or prices.

Figure 1 below indicates how many rules were associated with each category (or categories) of explanation. As the figure shows, 37 of the rules appeared to be "major" only because they were expected to produce $100 million in costs, $100 million in benefits, or both; 34 of the rules appeared to only involve some type of transfer (23 were increased transfers, 7 were decreased transfers, and 4 were non-federal transfers); 16 rules appeared to be major only because they were expected to result in increased costs or prices (but not at or above the $100 million threshold); 6 rules appeared to only involve "consumer surplus" issues; 4 rules appeared to only involve changes to fee structures; and 3 rules appeared to be major for multiple reasons.

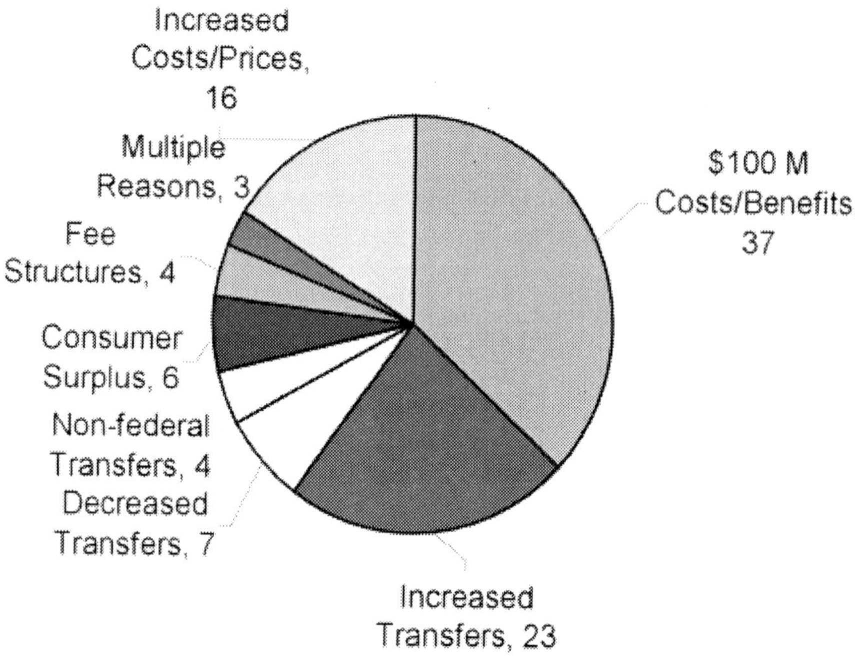

Source: CRS, based on information in GAO's major rule reports and the rules themselves.

Figure 1. The 100 Major Rules in Calendar Year 2010 Appear to Be "Major" for a Variety of Reasons.

Transfer Rules, Fee Rules, and Consumer Surplus Rules

As Table 3 and Figure 1 illustrate, the 100 major rules that were issued during calendar year 2010 appeared to have been considered "major" for a variety of reasons. Most of these rules appeared to be major because they were expected to have a $100 million annual "effect on the economy," but those effects sometimes seemed not directly related to expected regulatory compliance costs or the expected benefits of the rules.

Transfer Rules

For example, 37 of the 100 rules appeared to be "major" at least in part because they involved transfers of funds from one party to another party, most commonly the transfer of federal funds to the recipients of those funds (e.g., grants, food stamps, Medicare or Medicaid funds, special pay for members of the military, and crop payments).[24]

Increased Federal Transfers

In 23 of these transfer rules, the federal transfer payments appeared to be increasing. For example, see the following:

- A January 25, 2010, DOE rule on "Weatherization Assistance Program for Low-Income Persons" reduced the procedural burdens on evaluating applications from buildings that are part of HUD assisted and public housing programs, the Federal Low Income Housing Tax Credit Program, and the USDA Rural Development Program. DOE indicated that the $5 billion in grants provided under this program by the American Recovery and Reinvestment Act of 2009 (P.L. 111-5) made the rule a major rule, and "constitute transfer payments, meaning that they do not represent a change in the total resources available to society."[25]
- A January 29, 2010, USDA Food and Nutrition Service rule established new eligibility and certification requirements for the receipt of food stamps. USDA said that it expects this rule to simplify program administration, allow states greater flexibility, and provide enhanced access to eligible populations. The agency estimated that the total transfer costs to the government of this rule would be $2.669 billion in FY2010 and $13.541 billion during the five-year period from FY2010 through FY2014.[26]

- A March 12, 2010, rule issued by the Office of Innovation and Improvement within ED established priorities, requirements, definitions, and selection criteria under the Investing in Innovation Fund, which provides funding support to local educational agencies (LEAs) and nonprofit organizations in a partnership with one or more LEAs or a consortium of schools with a record of improving student achievement and attainment. ED estimated that the final rule would result in associated "annual monetized transfers" of $643 million per year from the federal government to LEAs and nonprofit organizations.[27]
- An April 16, 2010, DOD rule provided for retroactive stop loss special pay to members of the military service as authorized and appropriated in the Supplemental Appropriations Act, 2009 (Section 310 of P.L. 111-32). Although DOD did not provide a cost-benefit analysis with the final rule, in the preamble to the rule the department stated that the rule would have a $100 million annual impact on the economy in that the "Supplemental Appropriations Act, 2009 appropriated $534,400,000 to the Department of Defense, to remain available for obligation until expended."[28]
- A July 22, 2010, rule issued by the Centers for Medicare and Medicaid Services (CMS) within HHS announced the annual update to the hospice wage index for FY2011 and continued the phase out of the wage index budget neutrality adjustment factor. As a result, CMS estimated that total federal hospice payments would increase by $220 million in FY2010.[29]
- A July 30, 2010, rule issued by the Office of Consumer Information and Insurance Oversight (OCIIO) within HHS implemented Section 1101 of the Patient Protection and Affordable Care Act of 2010 (PPACA, P.L. 111-148, March 23, 2010), which required HHS to establish, either directly or through contracts with states or nonprofit entities, a temporary high-risk health insurance pool program to provide affordable health insurance coverage to uninsured individuals with pre-existing conditions. OCIIO estimated that the annual reporting and recordkeeping costs would be less than $2 million, but said that $5 billion in federal funds would be transferred from the Secretary to contractors to aid in administering the program from July 1, 2010, to December 31, 2013.[30]
- An August 31, 2010, DVA rule amended the department's adjudication regulations to implement the decision of the Secretary of

Veterans Affairs that there is a positive association between exposure to certain herbicides and the subsequent development of hairy cell leukemia and other chronic B-cell leukemias, Parkinson's disease, and ischemic heart disease. DVA estimated that the total cost for this rulemaking (primarily retroactive and ongoing benefits payments) to be $13.6 billion during FY2010, $25.3 billion for 5 years, and $42.2 billion over 10 years.[31]

- An October 25, 2010, rule issued by the Farm Service Agency (FSA) within USDA provided emergency assistance to reestablish the purchasing of rice, cotton, soybeans, and sweet potatoes in specified counties for which a disaster designation was issued based on excessive moisture and related conditions for the 2009 crop year. The rule specified the eligibility requirements, payment calculations, and application procedures for the Crop Assistance Program. FSA estimated that the total cost to the government for the program would be between $137 million and $543 million, depending on how many producers in disaster counties applied for payments.[32]

One other rule appeared to be "major" because federal loans were expected to be converted into transfer payments (which we coded as a transfer increase). On January 19, 2010, the Federal Emergency Management Agency (FEMA) within DHS published a rule that amended the agency's Special Community Disaster Loan (CDL) Program regulations to establish procedures and requirements for Special CDL cancellations. The cancellations were authorized by Section 4502(a) of the U.S. Troop Readiness, Veterans' Care, Katrina Recovery, and Iraq Accountability Appropriations Act, 2007 (P.L. 110-128). The Special CDL Program and the cancellation provisions applied to communities in the Gulf Coast region who received Special CDLs following Hurricanes Katrina and Rita. FEMA estimated that up to $1.3 billion in loans, interest, and costs could be forgiven under this effort.[33]

Decreased Federal Transfers

Nine other major rules appeared to be "major" at least in part because they were decreasing the amount of federal transfers provided.[34] For example, see the following:

- An August 12, 2010, CMS rule implemented a new prospective payment system for Medicare outpatient end-stage renal disease dialysis facilities, in compliance with the Medicare Improvements for

Patients and Providers Act of 2008 (P.L. 110-275). The rule also replaced the previous payment system and the methodologies for the reimbursement of separately billable outpatient end-stage renal disease services. CMS estimated that there would be an approximately $200 million decrease in payments to all end-stage renal disease facilities for renal dialysis during calendar year 2011, compared to what the payments would have been that year in the absence of this rule.[35]

- An August 16, 2010, CMS rule revised the Medicare hospital inpatient prospective payment systems (IPPS) for operating and capital-related costs of acute care hospitals to implement changes arising from the agency's continuing experience with these systems, and to implement certain statutory provisions.
- The rule also described the changes to the amounts and factors used to determine the rates for Medicare acute care hospital inpatient services for operating costs and capital-related costs, and updated the rate-of-increase limits for certain hospitals excluded from the IPPS that are paid on a reasonable cost basis subject to these limits. In addition, the rule updated the payment policy and the annual payment rates for the Medicare prospective payment system (PPS) for inpatient hospital services provided by long-term care hospitals (LTCHs) and set forth the changes to the payment rates, factors, and other payment rate policies under the LTCH PPS. CMS estimated that the final applicable percentage increase to the IPPS rates required by the statute, in conjunction with other final payment changes in the rule, would result in a $440 million decrease in FY2011 operating payments and an estimated $21 million decrease in FY2011 capital payments.[36]
- An October 15, 2010, DOD rule implemented Section 703 of the National Defense Authorization Act for Fiscal Year 2008, which stated that, with respect to any prescription filled on or after the date of enactment, the TRICARE Retail Pharmacy Program shall be treated as an element of DOD for purposes of procurement of drugs by federal agencies under 38 U.S.C. § 8126, to the extent necessary to ensure pharmaceuticals paid for by DOD that are provided by network retail pharmacies to TRICARE beneficiaries are subject to Federal Ceiling Prices (FCPs). Section 8126 established FCPs for covered drugs (requiring a minimum 24% discount) procured by DOD and three other agencies from manufacturers. DOD estimated that the rule would result in cost reductions from applying FCPs to the TRICARE

Retail Pharmacy Network in FY2010 through FY2015 of between $375 million and $560 million for Defense Health Program spending, and between $474 million and $707 million for Medicare-Eligible Retiree Health Care Fund spending.[37]

Non-Federal Transfers

Five major rules appeared to be "major" not because of increases or decreases in the transfer of federal funds, but because they were (at least in part) expected to result in annual transfers of $100 million or more from one population group to another.[38] Four of the rules were jointly issued by the Internal Revenue Service (IRS) within the Department of the Treasury, the Employee Benefits Security Administration (EBSA) within the Department of Labor, and CMS within the Department of Health and Human Services. For example, see the following:

- A February 2, 2010, rule required parity between mental health or substance use disorder benefits and medical/surgical benefits with respect to financial requirements and treatment limitations under group health plans and health insurance coverage offered in connection with a group health plan. The rule replaced regulations implementing the Mental Health Parity Act of 1996, and made conforming changes to reflect modifications to the act. The agencies said that the rule was considered "major" because total health care premiums were expected to rise 0.4%, and that increase was considered a transfer from those individuals not using mental health and substance use disorder benefits to those who do. The agencies estimated that those undiscounted transfers to be about $25.6 billion during the next 10 years.[39]
- A May 13, 2010, rule implemented the requirements for group health plans and health insurance issuers in the group and individual markets under provisions of the Patient Protection and Affordable Care Act regarding dependent coverage of children who have not reached age 26. Specifically, a plan or issuer that makes available dependent coverage of children was required to make such coverage available for children until attainment of 26 years of age. The agencies estimated the 2011 to 2013 transfers associated with this rule at between $3.5 and $6.9 billion, with the funds moving from individuals with family health insurance coverage who do not have

dependents aged 19-25 to those individuals with family health insurance coverage that do have such dependents.[40]

One other rule issued by the Commodity Credit Corporation within USDA also appeared to be a major rule because of these kinds of non-federal transfers.[41]

"Consumer Surplus" Rules and Rules Establishing Fees

Six of the 100 major rules appeared to be "major" because they were expected to trigger a certain type of economic activity by the public (termed a "consumer surplus").[42] All six of these rules were issued by DOI's Fish and Wildlife Service (FWS), and established hunting seasons and bag limits for certain types of migratory birds. For example, a September 23, 2010, FWS rule prescribed final late-season frameworks from which the states could select season dates, limits, and other options for the 2010-2011 migratory bird hunting seasons.[43] Based on an economic analysis prepared for an earlier season, FWS estimated that the rule would result in a consumer surplus of between $205 million and $270 million. The other five FWS rules had similar consumer surplus estimates.[44]

Four other rules appeared to be considered "major" because they established fee structures that were intended to fund certain government operations. For example, see the following:

- A June 16, 2010, NRC rule amended the licensing, inspection, and annual fees charged to the agency's applicants and licensees. NRC said it viewed these amendments as necessary to implement the Omnibus Budget Reconciliation Act of 1990, as amended (42 U.S.C. § 2214), which the agency said generally requires the NRC to recover through fees approximately 90% of its budget authority in FY2010. NRC determined that its required fee recovery amount for FY2010 was approximately $912.2 million and that, after accounting for billing adjustments, the total amount to be billed as fees was approximately $911.1 million.[45]
- A June 28, 2010, Department of State rule adjusted the Schedule of Fees for Consular Services based on an independent cost of service study's findings that the United States was not fully covering its costs for providing these services under the previous fee structure. The department said that it's primary objective was to ensure that fees for consular services reflected the costs to the United States of providing

the services to the extent possible. Among other things, the rule increased the Passport Book Application Services fee (for applicants age 16 and older) from $55 to $70, which was expected to produce additional fees of about $138 million. An increase in the Passport Book Security Surcharge from $20 to $40 was expected to generate additional fees of nearly $239 million.[46]

- A September 24, 2010, DHS rule adjusted the fee schedule for the U.S. Citizenship and Immigration Services to fully recover costs and maintain adequate service. DHS said that the rule would provide it with an average of $209 million in FY2010 and FY2011 annual fee revenue over the fee revenue that would have been collected under the previous fee structure. DHS said that the increased revenue would be used to fund the full cost of processing immigration benefit applications and associated support benefits, providing similar benefits to asylum and refugee applicants, and providing similar benefits to others at no charge.[47]

Expected Compliance Costs, Regulatory Benefits, or Both

Executive Order 12866 requires covered agencies (Cabinet departments and independent agencies, but not independent regulatory agencies) to prepare a cost-benefit analysis for any rule that is expected to be "economically significant."[48] According to OMB, the definition of an "economically significant" rule in the executive order is somewhat narrower than the definition of a "major rule" under the CRA (e.g., a $100 million annual "effect on the economy").[49] Also, Section 1 of the executive order states that:

> Costs and benefits shall be understood to include both quantifiable measures (to the fullest extent that these can be usefully estimated) and qualitative measures of costs and benefits that are difficult to quantify, but nevertheless essential to consider. Further, in choosing among alternative regulatory approaches, agencies should select those approaches that maximize net benefits (including potential economic, environmental, public health and safety, and other advantages; distributive impacts; and equity), unless a statute requires another regulatory approach.

Thirty-nine of the 100 major rules that were published during calendar year 1999 appeared to be "major" at least in part because they were expected to result in at least $100 million in annual compliance costs, $100 million in annual benefits, or both.[50] (Thirty of the rules were expected to have regulatory costs of at least $100 million, and 29 rules were expected to have regulatory benefits of at least $100 million.) In 20 of the 39 rules, estimated costs and benefits were both expected to exceed $100 million. In the 19 other major rules, the agencies did not provide a monetary estimate of either annual costs or benefits, or those estimates were less than $100 million.

In almost all of the rules in which both benefits and costs were estimated and monetized, the agencies' average or central estimates of regulatory benefits were larger than their average or central estimates of compliance costs. However, in some of these cases, the ranges of estimated benefits and costs overlapped, or could overlap. Therefore, while these rules appeared likely to produce net benefits, it is theoretically possible that the costs of the rules could exceed the benefits (assuming the agencies' estimates of the range of costs and benefits are accurate). For example, see the following:

- A February 9, 2010, rule issued by the Environmental Protection Agency (EPA) revised the primary nitrogen dioxide national ambient air quality standards. The rule established a new 1-hour standard at a level of 100 parts per billion, and established requirements for a nitrogen dioxide monitoring network that will include monitors at locations where maximum nitrogen dioxide concentrations are expected. Nevertheless, EPA estimated that the cost of the rule in the year 2020 would be between $270 million and $510 million (in 2006 dollars), and the estimated benefits that year would be between $120 million and $580 million (in 2006 dollars). Therefore, EPA said the rule could result in either positive or negative net benefits.[51]
- A March 3, 2010, EPA rule promulgated national emission standards for hazardous air pollutants for certain existing stationary compression ignition reciprocating internal combustion engines. The rule also promulgated national air standards for hazardous air pollutants for certain existing non-emergency stationary compression ignition engines. EPA estimated the total national capital cost for the final rule to be $744 million, with a total national annual cost of $373 million in 2013. EPA estimated the monetized benefits of the rule to be between $850 million and $2.3 billion in 2013. Therefore, if $478 million or more of the expected capital costs occur in 2013, the total estimated costs of the rule in that year would exceed the lowest estimated benefits.[52]

- A May 28, 2010, rule issued by the Federal Aviation Administration (FAA) within DOT amended the agency's regulations by adding equipage requirements and performance standards for Automatic Dependent Surveillance-Broadcast (ADS-B) Out avionics on aircraft operating in Classes A, B, and C airspace, as well as certain other specified classes of airspace within the U.S. National Airspace System. FAA said that the rule facilitated the use of ADS-B for aircraft surveillance by FAA and DOD air traffic controllers to safely and efficiently accommodate aircraft operations and the expected increase in demand for air transportation. The agency estimated that the undiscounted quantified benefits of the final rule ranged from $6.8 billion to $8.5 billion, and estimated the undiscounted incremental costs at between $3.3 billion and $7.0 billion.[53] Therefore, although average expected benefits substantially exceeded average expected costs, the highest estimate of cost ($7.0 billion) was slightly higher than the lowest estimate of benefits ($6.8 billion).
- A September 15, 2010, rule issued by the Civil Rights Division within DOJ revised the regulation that implements Title II of the Americans with Disabilities Act (ADA), relating to nondiscrimination on the basis of disability in state and local government services. The department reportedly issued this rule in order to adopt enforceable accessibility standards under the ADA that are consistent with the minimum guidelines and requirements issued by the Architectural and Transportation Barriers Compliance Board (Access Board), and to update or amend certain provisions of the Title II regulation so that they comport with the department's legal and practical experiences in enforcing the ADA since 1991. DOJ's estimate of compliance costs ranged from $12.8 billion to $25.8 billion, and the estimate of benefits ranged from $22.0 billion to $66.2 billion. Therefore, although average expected benefits substantially exceeded average expected costs, the highest estimate of cost ($25.8 billion) was higher than the lowest estimate of benefits ($22.0 billion).[54]

Net Benefits

In 14 of the 20 rules with estimated annual regulatory costs and benefits of at least $100 million, the agencies' *lowest* estimates of regulatory benefits were larger than the *highest* estimated compliance costs. Therefore, assuming that the agencies' estimates of the range of costs and benefits were correct, the rules should produce positive net benefits. For example, see the following:

- A March 9, 2010, DOE rule established energy conservation standards for small electric motors. The department estimated that the annualized costs of this rule would be about $264 million per year. DOE estimated a range of possible values for the total monetary benefits of this final rule from $867.5 million to about $1.36 billion.[55]
- A March 19, 2010, rule issued by the Food and Drug Administration (FDA) within HHS was identical to the provisions of the final rule on cigarettes and smokeless tobacco published by FDA in 1996, with certain required exceptions. The rule prohibited the sale of cigarettes and smokeless tobacco to individuals under the age of 18 and imposed specific marketing, labeling, and advertising requirements. Although FDA did not include a cost-benefit analysis in the 2010 rule, in the 1996 rule, the agency said that the rule could prevent 60,000 early deaths. The monetary value of these and other health benefits was estimated to be between $9.2 billion and $43 billion per year. FDA estimated the rule's overall compliance costs at from $174 million to $187 million in one-time costs, and from $149 million to $185 million in annual operating costs.[56] Therefore, even if the highest estimated one-time costs occurred in the same year as the highest estimated annual operating costs, the total would still be less than the lowest estimated benefits for that year.
- An April 5, 2010, rule issued by the Federal Motor Carrier Safety Administration (FMSCA) within DOT incorporated new performance standards for electronic on-board recorders (EOBRs) installed in commercial motor vehicles manufactured on or after June 4, 2012. The rule also made motor carriers that have demonstrated serious noncompliance with hours-of-service rules subject to mandatory installation of EOBRs meeting the new performance standards. FMSCA said that the costs of the final rule on an annualized basis over a 10-year period would be $139 million. FMCSA determined the benefits of the final rule to be $182 million annually, which included safety benefits of electronic onboard recorder use by estimating reductions in hours of service violations and resulting reductions in fatigue-related crashes.[57]
- An April 16, 2010, DOE rule amended the existing energy conservation standards for residential water heaters (other than tabletop and electric instantaneous models), gas-fired direct heating equipment, and gas-fired pool heaters. DOE determined that the annualized monetized benefits of the rule would be between $1.67

billion per year and $2.02 billion per year, with costs estimated to be between $1.25 billion per year and $1.28 billion per year.[58]

- An August 9, 2010, rule issued by the Occupational Safety and Health Administration (OSHA) within DOL revised the agency's "Cranes and Derricks Standard" and related sections of the "Construction Standard" to update and specify industry work practices necessary to protect employees during the use of cranes and derricks in construction. This rule also addressed advances in the designs of cranes and derricks, related hazards, and the qualifications of employees needed to operate them safely. OSHA estimated that the total annualized costs of the rule would be $154.1 million. OSHA estimated that the annual benefits included injuries prevented (175), fatalities prevented (22), and property damage from tipovers prevented ($7 million), for total monetized benefits of $209.3 million.[59]

Net Costs

In only one of the major rules did the agency indicate that the rule would likely result in net costs (i.e., that the highest estimate of benefits was less than the lowest estimate of costs). On January 15, 2010, the Federal Railroad Administration (FRA) within DOT issued a rule on "Positive Train Control Systems" that were required on certain passenger and freight rail lines by the Rail Safety Improvement Act of 2008 (P.L. 110-432, 122 Stat. 4854, October 16, 2008).[60] Congress enacted the statutory requirement in the wake of several serious rail accidents involving dozens of fatalities and hundreds of injuries. FRA estimated that the rule would reduce deaths and injuries from this type of accident by more than 50%, and estimated the monetized benefits of the rule at between $440 million and $674 million. However, the agency estimated the 20-year costs at between $9.5 billion and $13.2 billion—about 20 times greater than the estimated benefits. FRA noted this imbalance in the rule, but said it was "constrained by the requirements of [the Rail Safety Improvement Act of 2008], which do not provide latitude for implementing [positive train controls] differently."[61]

Monetized Costs but Non-monetized Benefits

In several other rules, the agencies estimated the annual compliance costs at $100 million or more, but provided only qualitative descriptions of expected regulatory benefits. Nevertheless, the agencies indicated in many of these rules that the value of the expected benefits, if monetized, would exceed or "justify" the costs. For example, see the following:

- A January 11, 2010, rule issued by the Securities and Exchange Commission (SEC) amended the custody and recordkeeping rules under the Investment Advisers Act of 1940 and related forms by providing additional safeguards when a registered adviser has custody of client funds or securities. The SEC estimated the aggregate compliance costs at more than $126 million; it said the non-monetized benefits would be "substantial," and would include increasing investors' confidence when obtaining advisory services from registered investment advisers, which could lead to more efficient allocation of investor assets and an increase in the availability of capital.[62]
- An April 14, 2010, FDA rule amended the agency's regulations on the use of ozone-depleting substances in self-pressurized containers to remove the essential-use designations for certain substances used in oral pressurized metered-dose inhalers (MDIs). As a result, the agency estimated that private, third-party, and public expenditures on inhaled medicines would increase by roughly $90 million to $280 million per year. FDA characterized the benefits as "environmental and public health improvements from protecting stratospheric ozone by reducing chlorofluorocarbons (CFCs) emissions" and "expectations of increased return on investments in environmentally friendly technology."[63]
- An October 29, 2010, ED rule amended the agency's regulations under certain programs (e.g., the Federal Family Education Loan (FFEL) Program, the William D. Ford Federal Direct Loan Program, and the Federal Pell Grant Program) to improve the integrity in these programs. The department indicated that annual paperwork-related costs could exceed $100 million,[64] but provided only qualitative descriptions of the expected benefits (e.g., "updated administrative structures for federal student aid programs," and "enhanced reliability and security of ability-to-benefit tests"). Nevertheless, ED stated in the rule that it believed "that the benefits of these regulations for students, consumers, and taxpayers justify the burdens of institutional compliance."[65]

Rules Expected to Result in Major Increases in Costs or Prices

Seventeen of the 100 major rules published in calendar year 2010 appeared to be "major rules" at least in part because they were expected to result in "major increase in costs or prices for consumers, individual industries, Federal, State, or local government agencies, or geographic regions."[66] CRS included rules in this category (instead of the earlier category of rules with a $100 million annual "effect on the economy") if those costs were either not monetized, or if they were estimated to be less than $100 million in any year. For example, see the following:

- A February 17, 2010, rule issued by the Agricultural Marketing Service (AMS) within USDA amended livestock and related provisions of the national organic program's regulations. The rule generally requires that producers maintain ruminant slaughter stock on pasture for each day that the finishing period corresponds with the grazing season for the geographical location. AMS did not monetize the benefits or the costs of the rule, but said that the benefits of the rule include uniformity in application to the livestock regulations especially as they relate to the pasturing of ruminants, which should result in a near elimination of violations of the pasture regulations. The agency said that the costs of the rule include an increase in the cost of production for producers who currently do not pasture their ruminant animals and those producers who do not manage their pastures at a sufficient level to provide at least 30% dry matter intake. AMS also said there may be an increase in consumer prices, but did not estimate the size of those increases.[67]
- A July 14, 2010, SEC rule addressed "pay to play" practices in investment advising, and prohibited an investment adviser from providing advisory services for compensation to a government client for two years after the adviser or certain of its executives or employees make a contribution to certain elected officials or candidates. The rule also prohibited an adviser from providing payment to any third party for a solicitation of advisory business from any government entity on behalf of such adviser, unless such third parties are registered broker-dealers or registered investment advisers. The SEC said that advisers with government clients would incur costs to monitor contributions and establish compliance procedures, and estimated initial compliance costs of approximately $2,352 per

smaller firm, $29,407 per medium firm, and $58,813 per larger firm. The Commission also estimated that the rule would impose annual, ongoing compliance expenses of approximately $2,940 per smaller firm, $117,625 per medium firm, and $235,250 per larger firm. In addition, the Commission estimated that advisers will incur an aggregate cost of approximately $200,246 per year and the non-labor costs of $20,080,000. The SEC did not monetize the expected benefits of the rule, but said it should (among other things) help minimize or eliminate manipulation of the market for advisory services to state and local governments.[68]

- A July 16, 2010, rule issued by the Employee Benefits Security Administration (EBSA) within DOL required that certain service providers to employee pension benefit plans disclose information to assist plan fiduciaries in assessing the reasonableness of contracts or arrangements, including the reasonableness of the service providers' compensation and potential conflicts of interest that may affect the service providers' performance. EBSA did not quantify the expected benefits of the rule, but said that mandatory proactive disclosure would reduce sponsor information costs, discourage harmful conflicts of interest, and enhance service value. EBSA estimated that the annual cost of this rule from 2011 to 2020 would be between $54.3 million and $58.7 million.[69]
- A July 28, 2010, rule issued by the Office of the Comptroller of the Currency within the Department of the Treasury and other agencies implemented provisions of the Secure and Fair Enforcement for Mortgage Licensing Act of 2008 (P.L. 110-289). The final rule required mortgage loan originators employed by national banks to register with the Nationwide Mortgage Licensing System and Registry and maintain their registration. Mortgage loan originators were also required to obtain a unique identifier through the registry that will remain with that originator, regardless of changes in employment. In addition, the rule required mortgage loan originators and national banks to provide these unique identifiers to consumers in certain circumstances, and requires national banks to adopt and follow written procedures to assure compliance with the registration requirements. Although the agencies indicated that these requirements would impose certain regulatory costs, they did not provide monetized estimates of those costs in the rule.[70]

"Major Rules" in Other Years

To determine whether our conclusions regarding major rules published during calendar year 2010 were consistent with other years and perspectives, CRS also examined the most recent edition of OMB's reports to Congress on the benefits and costs of federal regulations. OMB prepares these reports in accordance with the "Regulatory Right-to-Know Act,"[71] which requires the agency to identify the total annual benefits and costs of federal rules in the aggregate, by agency and agency program, and by "major rule." Although the act does not define the term "major rule," OMB has defined it as any rule (1) meeting the definition in the CRA (5 U.S.C. § 804(2), (2) meeting the analysis threshold in the Unfunded Mandates Reform Act (2 U.S.C. § 1532), or (3) designated as "economically significant" under Section 3(f) of Executive Order 12866. These three definitions overlap considerably, and any rule meeting the CRA definition is likely to be covered by the other two.[72]

According to the most recent "Regulatory Right-to-Know" report, which was issued in July 2010, OMB said that it concluded review of 66 major final rules during the 12-month period beginning October 1, 2008, and ending September 30, 2009.[73] Under Executive Order 12866, OMB does not review rules that are issued by independent regulatory agencies like the SEC and the NRC. However, OMB said that it used information from GAO's CRA database, and reported that independent regulatory agencies issued another 11 major final rules during this one-year period, bringing the total number of major rules discussed in the OMB report to 77.

Transfer Rules

OMB categorized 33 of the 77 major rules as "transfer rules" implementing federal budgetary programs, which OMB said primarily caused income transfers from taxpayers to program beneficiaries. In 22 of the 33 transfer rules, the agencies provided estimates of only the transfers themselves, which were almost always more than $100 million. In the other 11 transfer rules, the agencies provided no estimates of costs, benefits, or transfers, but OMB nonetheless categorized them as major rules. OMB reported that three other rules had transfer estimates of more than $100 million, with cost and benefits estimates that were always less than $100 million. Therefore, although OMB did not categorize these three rules as "transfers," a total of 36 rules (46.8% of the 77 rules) could be viewed as "major rules" either because of their OMB categorization as transfers, or because of the size of the transfers involved.

In three DOI/FWS migratory bird hunting rules, the agency only estimated the economic benefit (i.e., "consumer surplus") of the rules, all of which were more than $100 million. In 15 other major rules, the agencies provided monetary estimates of only regulatory costs. However, in 5 of these 15 rules, the estimates of regulatory costs were less than $100 million, and in 5 other rules issued by independent regulatory agencies, OMB did not report the size of the cost estimates.[74] In 9 other major rules (including 7 of the 11 rules issued by independent regulatory agencies), the agencies provided no monetized estimates of benefits or costs.

In 15 of the remaining 16 rules, OMB provided monetized estimates of both benefits and costs.[75] In 3 of these 15 rules, only the estimated benefits approached or exceeded $100 million. In contrast, none of the 15 rules had regulatory costs of at least $100 million that did not also have regulatory benefits at that level. In 12 of these 15 rules, the mid-point of the benefits estimate was greater than the mid-point of the cost estimate. Even when using the highest estimate of costs and the lowest estimates of benefits, 8 of the 15 rules were expected to produce positive net benefits. Alternatively, using the highest estimate of benefits and the lowest estimate of cost, all 15 rules were expected to produce positive net benefits.

These results regarding major rules issued during calendar years 2008 and 2009 appear to be consistent with our analysis of major rules issued during calendar year 2010. That is, rules seem to be considered "major" for a variety of reasons. The most common reason why OMB considered rules "major" was because of the transfer of federal funds, not because of the agencies' estimates of regulatory costs or benefits. Where rules appeared to be "major" because of estimated costs or benefits, the size of the estimated benefits were often larger.

Concluding Observations

The REINS Act, like the Congressional Review Act that it seeks to amend, is an attempt to reestablish a measure of congressional authority over agency rulemaking. The bill's supporters have asserted that the number of "major rules" that impose at least $100 million in annual costs on regulated entities has grown significantly in recent years. Because all agency rulemaking authority is delegated from Congress, supporters of the REINS Act assert that it is appropriate for Congress to vote on whether or not these major rules should take effect.

Number of Rules and Why Considered "Major"

While supporters and opponents of the REINS Act can vigorously debate the merits of a congressional approval process as contemplated in the legislation, the factual underpinnings of that debate should be as clear and agreed upon as possible. However, there appear to be some misconceptions regarding the number of major rules that have been issued in recent years, and why those rules were considered "major."

Several observers have said that the number of rules, and the number of major rules, has increased sharply during the Obama Administration.[76] An editorial in the *Wall Street Journal* stated that federal agencies had issued 59 major final rules in 2009 and 62 in 2010, up from an average of between 30 and 40 major rules in the previous 25 years.[77] However, GAO's federal rules database indicates that the number of major final rules has been at or above 50 in every full calendar year since the CRA was enacted in March 1996, and the number of major rules first exceeded 80 during the last calendar year of the George W. Bush Administration, when federal agencies issued 95 major rules. The number of major rules fell somewhat in 2009, the first year of the Obama Administration (to 84), but 11 of those rules appear to have been issued during the final days of the Bush Administration. In 2010, federal agencies published 100 major rules.

Also, although several observers have indicated that all major rules have annual costs of at least $100 million,[78] this report indicates that the major rules published in recent years appeared to be "major" for a variety of reasons. Many of the rules seemed to have been placed in that category because they substantially increased or decreased federal transfer payments—not because of expected regulatory compliance costs or benefits. Some observers may contend that at least some of these transfers are, in fact, regulatory costs (e.g., system-wide increases in the cost of health insurance, with the benefits flowing primarily from one group to another). Even under this view, however, those costs are somewhat different than compliance costs that are imposed upon particular industries or groups.

Of the major rules that had annual compliance cost estimates of $100 million or more, the rules frequently had estimated benefits that were much higher. In fact, in 14 of the major rules that were published in calendar year

2010, the agencies' highest estimated compliance costs were less than the lowest estimated benefits. In contrast, only one rule had estimated benefits that were lower than the lowest estimated costs (the DOT rule on "positive train control systems"), and in that rule the agency indicated that the costs were driven by the specific requirements in the underlying statute. In many other rules, the agencies provided monetized estimates of regulatory costs, but provided only qualitative descriptions of expected regulatory benefits. Other rules were expected to result in increased costs or prices, but the estimates for those increases were either less than $100 million or were not monetized.

Congressional Oversight

Although the reasons why certain rules are considered major appear to be more varied than just compliance costs, that fact does not bring into question the appropriateness of congressional oversight of agency regulations, or the appropriateness of considering the type of congressional approval process contemplated by the REINS Act. For example, see the following:

- If a major rule is expected to increase or decrease federal transfer payments by more than $100 million, Congress may want to examine and/or approve the manner in which those regulatory transfers are constructed to ensure that they are consistent with the intent of the underlying statute, and that they are sustainable in the current budgetary environment.
- If a major rule is expected to result in additional fee revenue, Congress may want to ensure that the fee structure is appropriate, and that the amount of fees expected to be derived from the regulatory change are neither too high nor too low to cover the costs of the governmental function being funded.
- If an agency indicates that a major rule is expected to result in regulatory costs that are substantially greater than the expected benefits (as appears to be the case in the "positive train control systems" rule), Congress may want to examine those estimates more closely, and may ultimately decide to prevent the rule from taking effect. Congress may also want to examine whether (as DOT indicated in the positive train control systems rule) the requirements in the underlying statute are, in fact, the source of the negative net benefits.

- On the other hand, if an agency indicates that a rule is expected to produce regulatory benefits well in excess of its expected costs, Congress may want to question the accuracy of those estimated benefits and costs. If Congress concludes that a rule will cost much more than the agency estimated, or will yield much lower estimated benefits, then Congress may decide not to approve the rule.

To carry out these kinds of congressional oversight actions, either as part of a disapproval action under the CRA, or as part of an approval action under the REINS Act, Congress may need particular types of expertise. For example, to determine whether a CMS rule has properly established prospective payment systems for hospitals and doctors, Congress may want to consult with experts in how such systems are constructed and operate. To determine whether EPA has properly estimated the future benefits of a rule, Congress may want to consult with experts in risk analysis to determine whether certain health benefits are likely to materialize. H.R. 214 (112th Congress), if enacted, may help provide some of the expertise that may be needed. The bill would create a Congressional Office of Regulatory Analysis (CORA), transferring to the director of that office the Comptroller General's responsibilities under the CRA. The CORA director would be required to prepare a report on each major rule, including potential benefits and costs and an analysis of less costly alternatives. In carrying out these and other functions, the director is permitted to procure temporary experts and consultants.

Statutory Requirements

In some cases, the agency issuing the rule appeared to have little or no discretion in determining whether or not the rule would be a "major rule." For example, see the following:

- DOE said the January 25, 2005, rule on weatherization assistance for low income persons was "major" because of the $5 billion in grants provided by the American Recovery and Reinvestment Act of 2009.
- DOD said its April 16, 2010, rule on retroactive stop loss special pay to members of the military service was "major" because of the more than $534 million authorized and appropriated for that purpose in the Supplemental Appropriations Act, 2009.
- The NRC said its June 16, 2010, was "major" because the Omnibus Budget Reconciliation Act of 1990, as amended, generally requires

the agency to recover through fees approximately 90% of its FY2010 budget authority through fees (about $900 million).

If a major rule that is of congressional concern is simply implementing statutory requirements, and the statute requires recurring rules, Congress may want to revisit those statutory requirements to prevent future major rules with the same types of effects.

Specificity of Statutory Rulemaking Authority

Finally, some observers have asserted that one way to prevent burdensome federal regulations is for Congress to be more specific in the statutes underlying those rules. Congress can assign regulatory responsibilities to federal agencies in any number of ways, and the manner in which Congress does so can determine the amount of discretion given to the agencies and, conversely, the amount of control that Congress retains for itself. When Congress requires that a regulation be issued or made effective by a particular date, that it contain certain substantive elements, and that the rule be developed following certain procedures, then the delegation of legislative rulemaking authority is somewhat limited and Congress retains a measure of control over the subsequent policymaking process.

However, specificity in the statutes underlying agency rules can also constrain the agencies from developing regulations that are most cost effective. For example, the Federal Railroad Administration rule on "positive train control systems" was the only major rule issued in 2010 that was clearly expected to produce negative net benefits. The agency said that the expected costs of the rule were about 20 times the expected benefits. FRA noted this imbalance in the rule, but said it was "constrained by the requirements of [the Rail Safety Improvement Act of 2008], which do not provide latitude for implementing [positive train controls] differently."[79]

APPENDIX. "MAJOR RULES" FROM CALENDAR YEAR 2010

Table A-1. Chronological Listing of "Major Rules" from Calendar Year 2010 That Would Have Been Covered by the REINS Act

Agency	Title of Rule (RIN)	Date Published	Cost-Benefit Analysis Information Provided in GAO Report
Department of Energy	Energy Conservation Program: Energy Conservation Standards for Certain Consumer Products (Dishwashers, Dehumidifiers, Microwave Ovens, and Electric and Gas Kitchen Ranges and Ovens) and for Certain Commercial and Industrial Equipment (Commercial Clothes Washers) (1904-AB93)	1/8/2010	DOE considered the cost and benefits of the rule and determined that the costs outweigh the benefits. The benefits include energy savings, life cycle costs (LCC) savings for CCW consumers, positive national net present value, and emissions reductions. The costs include loss of manufacturer industry net present value and LCC increases for some CCW consumers. [DOE indicated in the preamble to the rule that it was expected to result in losses to manufacturers of less than $10 million, but the net present value of consumer benefits were estimated to be between $400 million and $900 million (in 2008 dollars).]
Securities and Exchange Commission	Custody of Funds or Securities of Clients by Investment Advisers (3235-AK32)	1/11/2010	The Commission analyzed the potential costs and benefits of the final rule. Though the Commission states the benefits to investors may be hard to quantify, it believes that the benefits will be substantial, including, generally, increasing investors' confidence when obtaining advisory services from registered investment advisers.

Table A-1. (Continued)

Agency	Title of Rule (RIN)	Date Published	Cost-Benefit Analysis Information Provided in GAO Report
Securities and Exchange Commission			In addition, the Commission believes the amendments to the rule could, to a limited extent, promote efficiency and capital formation as a result of such increased investor confidence. In particular, the Commission states that increased investor confidence could lead to more efficient allocation of investor assets, which could result in an increase in the assets under management of investment advisers and, depending on how those assets are invested, a potential increase in the availability of capital. Additionally, the Commission anticipates that investment advisers will find it easier to understand and comply with the rule as a result of the amendments, which may result in cost savings for advisers. The Commission believes the amendments will improve the clarity of the rule by adding several definitions. The Commission estimates that the aggregate costs for complying with the amendments to the final rule and related forms will be $126,278,204. Of this amount, the Commission estimates that $1,195,000 is a one-time computer system programming cost related to account statement legends, while the remainder will be recurred on an annual basis. The recurring costs under the rule are for the surprise examinations, internal control reports, and the burden hours associated with the changes to two related forms.

Agency	Title of Rule (RIN)	Date Published	Cost-Benefit Analysis Information Provided in GAO Report
Department of Housing and Urban Development	HOPE for Homeowners Program; Statutory Transfer of Program Authority to HUD and Conforming Amendments To Adopt Recently Enacted Statutory Changes (2502-AI76)	1/12/2010	According to the Department of Housing and Urban Development (HUD), it did not prepare an analysis of the costs and benefits of this interim rule. HUD did prepare an Economic Analysis for this rule. [The economic analysis reads as follows: HUD found that the economic impacts from the changes in this interim rule stem largely from increased participation in the H4H program. HUD estimates that, with 10,000 participants annually, the H4H program will generate $273 million in net benefits to society and that H4H participation could be as high as 137,500 households over the life of the program, with commensurately higher benefits.]
Department of Transportation, Federal Railroad Administration	Positive Train Control Systems (2130-AC03)	1/15/2010	The Federal Railroad Administration (FRA) analyzed the costs and benefits of this final rule. The costs FRA anticipates to accrue from adopting this final rule include: (1) costs associated with developing implementation plans and administrative functions related to the implementation and operation of positive train control (PTC) systems, including the information technology and communication systems that make up the central office; (2) hardware costs for onboard locomotive system components, including installation; (3) hardware costs for wayside system components, including installation; and (4) maintenance costs for all system components.

Table A-1. (Continued)

Agency	Title of Rule (RIN)	Date Published	Cost-Benefit Analysis Information Provided in GAO Report
Department of Transportation, Federal Railroad Administration			FRA estimates the total 20-year discounted costs to be $13,205,614,091 at a 3-percent discount rate and $9,547,522,721 at a 7-percent discount rate. FRA expects two types of benefits to result from the implementation of this final rule—benefits from railroad accident reduction and business benefits from efficiency gains. The first type would include safety benefits or savings expected to accrue from the reduction in the number and severity of casualties arising from train accidents that would occur on lines equipped with PTC systems. FRA estimates the total 20-year discounted benefits to be $673,801,919 at a 3-percent discount rate and $439,705,397 at a 7-percent discount rate.
Federal Reserve System and Federal Trade Commission	Fair Credit Reporting Risk- Based Pricing Regulations (3084-AA94)	1/15/2010	The Federal Reserve System (the Board) and Federal Trade Commission (the Commission) (collectively, the agencies) analyzed the costs and benefits of this final rule. According to the Commission, the estimated average annual labor cost for all categories of entities covered by this final rule will be $252,048,000 or $1,263 per covered entity.

Agency	Title of Rule (RIN)	Date Published	Cost-Benefit Analysis Information Provided in GAO Report
Federal Reserve System and Federal Trade Commission			The benefits of this final rule identified by the Commission include: (1) educating consumers about the role that their consumer reports play in the pricing of credit; and (2) alerting consumers to the existence of potentially negative information in their consumer reports so that they may check their reports and correct any inaccurate information. The Commission expects more consumers will check their credit reports because of the rule, which will result in improving the accuracy of credit reports generally. Thus, the Commission believes that the benefits of the rule substantially outweigh the costs to those engaged in risk-based pricing.
Department of Homeland Security, Federal Emergency Management Agency	Special Community Disaster Loans Program (1660-AA44)	1/19/2010	FEMA determined that the overall cost impact of this rule is the cost to the applicant to apply for the cancellation, as well as the impact on the economy of potentially forgiving all Special Community Disaster Loans (CDLs) and any related interest and costs. FEMA estimated that the annual estimated cost to submit the application for loan cancellation will be $4,850.32. FEMA determined that if all 152 recipients of Special CDLs apply for and are found eligible for full cancellation under the rule, up to $1,270,501,241, plus any applicable interests and costs, could be forgiven.

Table A-1. (Continued)

Agency	Title of Rule (RIN)	Date Published	Cost-Benefit Analysis Information Provided in GAO Report
Department of Homeland Security, Federal Emergency Management Agency			Therefore, the maximum total economic impact of this final rule was determined by FEMA to be approximately $1.3 billion. However, FEMA notes that it is impossible to predict the economic impact with precision because it cannot know the dollar amounts or number of loans that will be cancelled. Also, although the impact of the final rule may be spread over multiple years as applications are received, processed, and loans cancelled, the total economic effects of a specific loan cancellation would only occur once, rather than annually.
Department of Energy	Weatherization Assistance Program for Low-Income Persons (1904-AB97)	1/25/2010	DOE prepared a cost-benefit analysis in conjunction with the final rule. DOE states that the American Recovery and Reinvestment Act of 2009 provided $5 billion for the weatherization program, and that the grants provided under this program constitute transfer payments, meaning that they do not represent a change in the total resources available to society. DOE states that the final rule will have the benefit of improving weatherization. DOE acknowledges that the final rule could impact the process used by grantees and subgrantees to evaluate applications with respect to multi-unit buildings for the purpose of distributing funds provided under the Recovery Act, and that could potentially result in a change of the distribution of funding.

Agency	Title of Rule (RIN)	Date Published	Cost-Benefit Analysis Information Provided in GAO Report
Department of the Treasury, Office of the Comptroller of the Currency; Federal Reserve System; Federal Deposit Insurance Corporation; Department of the Treasury, Office of Thrift Supervision	Risk-Based Capital Guidelines; Capital Adequacy Guidelines; Capital Maintenance: Regulatory Capital; Impact of Modifications to Generally Accepted Accounting Principles; Consolidation of Asset-Backed Commercial Paper Programs; and Other Related Issues (1557-AD26, 3064-AD48, 1550-AC36)	1/28/2010	In its submission to the Comptroller General, the agencies did not include a cost-benefit analysis of the final rule. [In the preamble to the rule, the agencies stated that the rule (among other things) "eliminates the exclusion of certain consolidated asset-backed commercial paper programs from risk-weighted assets." Affected parties indicated that this and other changes in the rule could increase the cost of lending to consumers and businesses.]
Department of Agriculture, Food and Nutrition Service	Food Stamp Program: Eligibility and Certification Provisions of the Farm Security and Rural Investment Act of 2002 (0584- AD30)	1/29/2010	The Department of Agriculture (USDA) analyzed the costs. USDA estimates that the total costs to the government of this rule to be $2.669 billion in fiscal year 2010 and $13.541 billion over the 5 years fiscal year 2010 through fiscal year 2014. [In the preamble to the rule, USDA indicated that the first-year costs would be less than $70 million, and costs would be less than $5 million in each subsequent year.]

Table A-1. (Continued)

Agency	Title of Rule (RIN)	Date Published	Cost-Benefit Analysis Information Provided in GAO Report
Department of the Treasury, Internal Revenue Service; Department of Labor, Employee Benefits Security Administration; Department of Health and Human Services, Centers for Medicare and Medicaid Services	Interim Final Rules Under the Paul Wellstone and Pete Domenici Mental Health Parity and Addiction Equity Act of 2008 (1545-BJ05; 1210-AB30; 0938-AP65)	2/2/2010	The Departments analyzed the costs and benefits of the rule. According to the Departments, the costs include costs associated with increased utilization of mental health and substance use disorder benefits and costs associated with cumulative financial requirements and quantitative treatment limitations, including deductibles. Additionally, the Departments include compliance review costs and costs associated with MHPAEA disclosures. The Departments expect that the largest benefit associated with MHPAEA and these regulations will be derived from applying parity to cumulative quantitative treatment limitations such as annual or lifetime day or visit limits (visit limitations) to help ensure that vulnerable populations—those accessing substantial amounts of mental health and substance use disorder services—have better access to appropriate care. The Departments cannot estimate how large this benefit will be, because sufficient data is not available to estimate the number of covered individuals that had their benefits terminated because they reached their coverage limit. The Departments state that another potential benefit associated with MHPAEA and these regulations is that use of mental health and substance use disorder benefits could improve.

Agency	Title of Rule (RIN)	Date Published	Cost-Benefit Analysis Information Provided in GAO Report
Department of the Treasury, Internal Revenue Service; Department of Labor, Employee Benefits Security Administration; Department of Health and Human Services, Centers for Medicare and Medicaid Services			The Departments note that the finding that treatment can help increase the productivity of those suffering from mental illness suggests that increasing access to treatment of mental disorders could have a beneficial impact on lost productivity cost and lost earnings that stem from untreated and under treated mental health conditions and substance use disorders. The Departments, however, do not have sufficient data to determine whether this result will occur, and, if it does, the extent to which lost productivity cost and lost earnings could improve. According to the Departments, because expenditures on mental health and substance use disorder benefits only comprise 3–6 percent of the total benefits covered by a group health plan and 8 percent of overall healthcare costs, the Departments expect that group health plans will lower cost-sharing on mental health and substance use disorder benefits instead of raising cost-sharing on medical/surgical benefits.
Environmental Protection Agency	Primary National Ambient Air Quality Standards for Nitrogen Dioxide (2060-AO19)	2/9/2010	EPA prepared a regulatory impact analysis of the potential costs and benefits associated with the final rule. However, the Clean Air Act and judicial decisions do not permit EPA to consider the economic and technical feasibility of attaining ambient air standards, so EPA did not consider the results of the cost-benefit analysis in developing the final rule.

Table A-1. (Continued)

Agency	Title of Rule (RIN)	Date Published	Cost-Benefit Analysis Information Provided in GAO Report
Environmental Protection Agency			[According to the regulatory impact analysis for the rule, EPA estimated that in 2020, the costs would be between $270 million and $510 million, and the monetized benefits would be between $120 million and $580 million (all in 2006 dollars).]
Department of Agriculture, Agricultural Marketing Service	National Organic Program; Access to Pasture (Livestock) (0581-AC57)	2/17/2010	AMS considered the cost and benefits of the rule. AMS notes that the benefits include uniformity in application to the livestock regulations especially as they relate to the pasturing of ruminants, which will create equitable, consistent performance standards for all ruminant livestock producers and allow the accredited certifying agents (ACAs) and AMS to administer the livestock regulations in a way that reflects consumer preferences regarding the production of organic livestock and their products. AMS states that an additional benefit of uniform application of the NOP livestock regulations should result in a near elimination of violations of the pasture regulations. AMS believes this will eliminate the filing of complaints regarding the pasturing of ruminants. AMS states that the costs include an increase in the cost of production for producers who currently do not pasture their ruminant animals and those producers who do not manage their pastures at a sufficient level to provide at least 30 percent DMI.

Agency	Title of Rule (RIN)	Date Published	Cost-Benefit Analysis Information Provided in GAO Report
Department of Agriculture, Agricultural Marketing Service			AMS notes the costs associated with complying with this rule would vary based on the livestock producer's current practices and the degree to which they conform to the amended livestock regulations. Additionally, AMS believes ruminant livestock operations currently pasturing their animals may see minimal increased costs, if any. According to AMS, the potential costs include land and seed for pasture and costs associated with providing sufficient vegetation for grazing throughout the grazing season, which would include the time (labor) spent seeding the pastures, fuel for equipment used in seeding, and the cost of seed. AMS believes costs of pasture vary depending on location, with costs likely being higher for certified organic pasture. AMS also believes seed costs will vary depending on what is to be grown and how many acres are to be grown. AMS states such costs may be offset by the benefits of using improved pasture, which include a lower cost of purchased feed (grains and forages) per hundredweight of milk or meat produced, reduced forage harvest costs, and reduced veterinary costs. Also, AMS notes that at the retail level, there may be increased consumer prices.

Table A-1. (Continued)

Agency	Title of Rule (RIN)	Date Published	Cost-Benefit Analysis Information Provided in GAO Report
Department of Agriculture, Agricultural Marketing Service			AMS believes for organic slaughter stock producers, an increase in costs might result in a greater volume of slaughter animals, at least in the short term, entering the market driving down prices. Additionally, AMS states that longer term these increased costs could result in increased consumer prices unless the increased costs are offset by reductions in other costs of production. AMS states other costs of production that could be expected to go down are costs associated with producer harvest and purchase of feed and the cost of herd health. AMS also notes that dairy producers not currently pasturing their animals and those not managing their pastures at a level sufficient to provide at least 30 percent DMI are also expected to experience increased costs, which could, at least in the short term, lead to a reduced organic milk supply.
Federal Reserve System	Truth in Lending (Docket No. R-1370)	2/22/2010	The Board did not perform a cost-benefit analysis in conjunction with the final rule. [In the rule summary, FRS stated that the rule "establishes a number of new substantive and disclosure requirements to establish fair and transparent practices pertaining to open-end consumer credit plans, including credit card accounts.

Agency	Title of Rule (RIN)	Date Published	Cost-Benefit Analysis Information Provided in GAO Report
Federal Reserve System			In particular, the rule limits the application of increased rates to existing credit card balances, requires credit card issuers to consider a consumer's ability to make the required payments, establishes special requirements for extensions of credit to consumers who are under the age of 21, and limits the assessment of fees for exceeding the credit limit on a credit card account."]
Environmental Protection Agency	National Emission Standards for Hazardous Air Pollutants for Reciprocating Internal Combustion Engines (2060- AP36)	3/3/2010	EPA performed a cost-benefit analysis in conjunction with the final rule. EPA determined that the air quality impacts of the final rule would be to reduce total hazardous air pollutant (HAP) emissions from stationary reciprocating internal combustion engines (RICE) by 1,010 tons per year (tpy) beginning in 2013. The final rule is expected to reduce other pollutants, such as carbon monoxide (by 14,000 tpy in 2013), fine particulate matter (PM) (by 2,800 tpy in 2013), and volatile organic compounds (VOC) (by 27,000 in 2013). The final rule will also reduce emissions of sulfur oxide through the use of ultra low sulfur diesel (ULSD) fuel by zero to 31,000 tpy in 2013, depending on the number of engines that used ULSD prior to the enactment of the final rule. EPA estimated the total national capital cost for the final rule for existing stationary RICE to be $744 million, with a total national annual cost of $373 million in 2013.

Table A-1. (Continued)

Agency	Title of Rule (RIN)	Date Published	Cost-Benefit Analysis Information Provided in GAO Report
Environmental Protection Agency			EPA estimated the monetized benefits of the rule, which it calculated in terms of the co-benefits associated with reducing PM, to be between $940 million and $2.3 billion (using a 3-percent discount rate) or between $850 million and $2.1 billion (using a 7-percent discount rate) in 2013.
Securities and Exchange Commission	Money Market Fund Reform (3235-AK33)	3/4/2010	The Securities and Exchange Commission (the Commission) analyzed the costs and benefits of this final rule and concluded that the benefits justify the costs. The Commission believes that the benefits of this rule include reducing money market funds' exposure to credit, interest rate, and liquidity risks, among other benefits. The Commission also recognized that this rule may cause the yields of funds to decrease in some circumstances, among other costs..... The Commission determined that this final rule contains three new information collections requirements and revises three existing information collection requirements under the Act. The Commission has submitted these information collection requirements to the Office of Management and Budget (OMB) for review... The Commission estimates that the total burden hours associated with the amendments to the 2a-7 information collection requirement will increase the renewal estimate to 395,779 hours annually.

Agency	Title of Rule (RIN)	Date Published	Cost-Benefit Analysis Information Provided in GAO Report
Securities and Exchange Commission			The Commission estimates that the total annual burden associated with the 22e-3 information collection for all money market funds and conduit funds will be approximately 110 minutes. The Commission estimates that the total annual burden associated with Form N-MFP information collection will be 94,189 burden hours, on average, for all money market funds in the first three years. Finally, the Commission estimates that the total annual burden associated with the 30b1-6T information collection will be 2,100 hours for all money market funds required to submit portfolio schedules.
Department of Energy	Energy Conservation Program: Energy Conservation Standards for Small Electric Motors (1904-AB70)	3/9/2010	The Department of Energy (DOE) analyzed the costs and benefits of this final rule. DOE estimated that the annualized costs of this rule to be $263.9 million per year at a 7-percent discount rate and $263.7 million per year at a 3-percent discount rate. DOE estimated a range of possible values for the total monetary benefits of this final rule, depending on the discount rate, low versus high energy prices, and other factors. DOE's lowest estimate of the benefits of this rule is $867.5 million and its highest estimate is $1,358.8 million.

Table A-1. (Continued)

Agency	Title of Rule (RIN)	Date Published	Cost-Benefit Analysis Information Provided in GAO Report
Securities and Exchange Commission	Amendments to Regulation SHO (3235-AK35)	3/10/2010	The Securities and Exchange Commission (the Commission) evaluated the costs and benefits of this final rule. The Commission identified various benefits of this rule, including promoting capital formation and restoring investor confidence in the securities market. The Commission believes that this rule's approach strikes the appropriate balance between preventing short selling—including potentially manipulative or abusive short selling—from being used as a tool to exacerbate a declining market in a security and the continued smooth functioning of the markets, including the provision of liquidity and price efficiency. The Commission believes that the rule will have minimal, if any, impact on market liquidity, price efficiency, and quote depths. The Commission estimates that this rule will have an average one-time initial cost of \$86,880 per self regulating organization (SRO) trading center and \$68,381 per non-SRO trading center required to establish the written policies and procedures under this rule. The Commission also estimates an average annual on-going cost of \$18,588 per trading center to ensure that the written policies and procedures are up-to-date and remain in compliance.

Agency	Title of Rule (RIN)	Date Published	Cost-Benefit Analysis Information Provided in GAO Report
Securities and Exchange Commission			In addition, the Commission estimates an average annual cost of $102,768 per trading center for on-going monitoring for and enforcement of trading in compliance with the rule. The Commission also estimates that this rule will have an average one-time initial cost of $68,381 per broker-dealer establishing the written policies and procedures under the rule. The Commission estimates an average annual on-going cost of $18,588 per broker-dealer to ensure that written policies and procedures are up-to-date and remain in compliance. In addition, the Commission estimates an average annual cost of $102,768 per brokerdealer for on-going monitoring for and enforcement of trading.
Department of Education	Investing in Innovation Fund (1855-AA06)	3/12/2010	Education believes that the costs associated with the final rule would be limited to the paperwork burden related to preparing an application, and that the benefits of the rule would outweigh any costs incurred by applicants. Education believes that the benefits of the final rule would be priorities, requirements, definitions, and selection criteria that would result in the selection of high-quality applications that are most likely to have a significant national impact on educational reform and improvement. Education estimates that the final rule will result in associated expenditures of $643 million from the federal government to local educational agencies (LEAs) and nonprofit organizations.

Table A-1. (Continued)

Agency	Title of Rule (RIN)	Date Published	Cost-Benefit Analysis Information Provided in GAO Report
Department of Health and Human Services, Food and Drug Administration	Regulations Restricting the Sale and Distribution of Cigarettes and Smokeless Tobacco To Protect Children and Adolescents (0910-AG33)	3/19/2010	In its current submission to the Comptroller General, the FDA did not include a cost-benefit analysis of the final regulations under this Act. [In the preamble, FDA referenced an earlier rule in which the agency estimated the annual costs at between $174 million and $187 million, and monetized the health benefits (e.g., 60,000 premature deaths avoided) at between $28 billion and $43 billion per year.]
Environmental Protection Agency	Regulation of Fuels and Fuel Additives: Changes to Renewable Fuel Standard Program (2060-AO81)	3/26/2010	The Environmental Protection Agency (EPA) analyzed the costs and benefits of this final rule. In its Regulatory Impact Analysis for this rule, EPA estimated the impacts of an expansion of renewable fuel use as required by this rule, but did not evaluate to what extent such an expansion would have occurred in the absence of this rule. EPA estimated that the 2022 impact on gasoline costs would be -2.4 cents per gallon; on diesel costs, -12.1 cents per gallon; on overall fuel costs, -$11.8 billion; and on gasoline and diesel consumption, -13.6 billion gallons. EPA also estimated that the total capital costs through 2022 would be $90.5 million. The estimated food costs would be 8.2 percent for corn, 10.3 percent for soybeans, and $10 per capita.

Agency	Title of Rule (RIN)	Date Published	Cost-Benefit Analysis Information Provided in GAO Report
Environmental Protection Agency			EPA estimated the economic impacts of this rule to be S2.6 billion for energy security, between -$630 million and -$2.2 billion for monetized health impacts, between S600 million and $12.2 billion for monetized greenhouse gases impacts, -$41.5 billion in oil impacts, 3.6 billion in farm gate food, $13 billion in farm income, -$57 million in corn exports, and -$453 million in soybean exports. EPA estimates the total benefit for this rule in 2022 to be between $13 billion and $26 billion.
Department of Justice, Drug Enforcement Administration	Electronic Prescriptions for Controlled Substances (1117- AA61)	3/31/2010	DEA performed a cost-benefit analysis in conjunction with the final rule. DEA estimates that the total annual costs will be: for practitioners' offices: $30,244,615, using a 7-percent discount rate ($29,602,769 using a 3-percent discount rate); for hospitals: $6,241,658 using a 7-percent discount rate ($5,352,737 using a 3-percent discount rate); for pharmacies: $2,026,046 using a 7-percent discount rate ($1,936,927 using a 3-percent discount rate); and for application providers: $4,817,509 using a 7-percent discount rate ($4,886,478 using a 3-percent discount rate). DEA estimates that the total annualized costs associated with the interim final rule will be $43,328,829 using a 7-percent discount rate ($41,778,910 using a 3-percent discount rate).

Table A-1. (Continued)

Agency	Title of Rule (RIN)	Date Published	Cost-Benefit Analysis Information Provided in GAO Report
Department of Justice, Drug Enforcement Administration			DEA estimates that the annualized gross benefits of the final rule from eliminating a number of callbacks to clarify prescriptions from pharmacies to doctors will be $419,745,516 using a 7-percent discount rate ($438,502,110 using a 3-percent discount rate). The interim final rule could also reduce the patient's wait time at the pharmacy, which DEA estimates will provide annualized savings over 15 years of $1 billion using a 7-percent discount ($1.03 billion using a 3- discount). However, the estimate for public wait time is an upper bound, and DEA did not include it in the primary estimate for the benefits of the interim final rule. The interim final rule will also allow pharmacies to eliminate file cabinets currently used to store original prescriptions for 2 years, which DEA estimates will provide a cost-savings for pharmacies of $1.38 million using a 7-percent discount rate ($1.4 million using a 3-percent discount rate). DEA also lists other benefits, which it did not attempt to quantify or monetize. DEA believes the interim final rule will directly affect drug diversion effectuated through stealing prescription pads, altering legitimate prescriptions, or altering a record at a pharmacy to hide diversion from pharmacy stock. DEA also believes that the interim final rule will help reduce adverse drug events that result from medication errors.

Agency	Title of Rule (RIN)	Date Published	Cost-Benefit Analysis Information Provided in GAO Report
Federal Reserve System	Electronic Fund Transfers (Docket No. R-1377)	4/1/2010	The Board did not perform a cost-benefit analysis in conjunction with the final rule. [In the rule summary, FRS stated that the rule "restricts a person's ability to impose dormancy, inactivity, or service fees for certain prepaid products, primarily gift cards. The final rule also, among other things, generally prohibits the sale or issuance of such products if they have an expiration date of less than five years. The amendments implement statutory requirements set forth in the Credit Card Accountability Responsibility and Disclosure Act of 2009."]
Department of Education	Race to the Top Fund (1810- AB10)	4/2/2010	Education determined that this interim final rule will not impose additional costs to state applicants, grantees, or the federal government. A state applicant may take additional time to create or revise its Race to the Top budget so that it conforms to the required budget range if the state had intended to request more than the maximum in the range. However, Education believes that the benefits outweigh any potential burden that the interim final rule may cause. [In the preamble to the rule, DOEd stated that the fund "seeks to spur reform of the country's education system," and that the final rule was issued without prior public comments "in order to make timely grant awards with ARRA funds."]

Table A-1. (Continued)

Agency	Title of Rule (RIN)	Date Published	Cost-Benefit Analysis Information Provided in GAO Report
Department of Transportation, Federal Motor Carrier Safety Administration	Electronic On-Board Recorders for Hours-of- Service Compliance (2126-AA89)	4/5/2010	FMCSA performed a cost-benefit analysis in conjunction with the final rule. FMCSA determined that the costs of the final rule on an annualized basis over a 10-year horizon will be $139 million. The costs analysis estimates the cost of carriers coming into compliance with the hours of service rules, and includes the electronic on-board recorders required to be compliant with the rule, as well as training time costs for drivers, administrative staff, and state enforcement personnel. FMCSA determined the benefits of the final rule to be $182 million annually, which includes safety benefits of electronic onboard recorder use by estimating reductions in hours of service violations and resulting reductions in fatigue-related crashes.
Department of Defense, Office of the Secretary	TRICARE; Relationship Between the TRICARE Program and Employer-Sponsored Group Health Coverage (0720-AB17)	4/9/2010	DoD completed an estimated annual impact analysis. An updated analysis of DoD's cost and population data for FY2009 indicates that the average MHS cost per active duty family members (NADFM) user under age 65 was $3,975 (in FY2009 dollars). After adjusting for inflation to FY2010, DoD estimates that the current year (FY2010) cost per NADFM user is $4,293. Multiplying this cost per user by the 14,921 NADFMs who would shift to OHI rather than using TRICARE, due to section 707, yields an annual estimated cost impact of $64.1 million in savings for Fiscal Year 2010.

Agency	Title of Rule (RIN)	Date Published	Cost-Benefit Analysis Information Provided in GAO Report
Department of Defense, Office of the Secretary			Based on a trend of 7-percent inflation offset by a projected 2-percent annual decrease in non-active duty family members under age 65, DoD estimates the following impact: $64.1 million in savings for Fiscal Year 2010; $67.3 million in savings for Fiscal Year 2011; $70.6 million in savings for Fiscal Year 2012; $74.2 million in savings for Fiscal Year 2013; $77.9 million in savings for Fiscal Year 2014; and $81.8 million in savings for Fiscal Year 2015.
Department of Health and Human Services, Food and Drug Administration	Use of Ozone-Depleting Substances; Removal of Essential-Use Designation (Flunisolide, etc.) (0910-AF92)	4/14/2010	The Food and Drug Administration (FDA) analyzed the costs and benefits of this final rule. According to FDA, the benefits of this rule include environmental and public health improvements from protecting stratospheric ozone by reducing chlorofluorocarbons (CFCs) emissions. FDA also expect the benefits to include expectations of increased returns on investments in environmentally friendly technology and continued international cooperation to comply with the spirit of the Montreal Protocol, thereby potentially reducing future emissions of ozone-depleting substances (ODSs) throughout the world. FDA determined that the costs of the final rule would include increased spending for needed medicines used to treat asthma and Chronic Obstructive Pulmonary Disease (COPD). FDA determined that the social costs of the final rule include the health benefits lost through decreased use of medicines that may result from increased prices.

Table A-1. (Continued)

Agency	Title of Rule (RIN)	Date Published	Cost-Benefit Analysis Information Provided in GAO Report
Department of Health and Human Services, Food and Drug Administration			FDA was unable to quantify the economic costs of reducing the variety of marketed products from which consumers, and their doctors, can choose. FDA estimated that, depending on whether asthma and COPD patients use the most or least expensive of alternatives, private, third-party, and public expenditures on inhaled medicines would increase by roughly $90 million to $280 million per year.
Department of Health and Human Services, Centers for Medicare & Medicaid Services	Medicare Program; Policy and Technical Changes to the Medicare Advantage and the Medicare Prescription Drug Benefit Programs (0938-AP77)	4/15/2010	The Centers for Medicare & Medicaid Services (CMS) analyzed the costs and benefits of this final rule. CMS estimated the costs and savings of this rule for calendar years 2010 through 2015. CMS estimates that the total cost of this rule in calendar year 2010 will be approximately $260.3 million, and that the rule will have a total net savings over the 6-year period 2010 to 2015 of $341.70 million. CMS also predicts that this rule will improve coordination of care, increase quality of data reporting, increase ability to comply with existing regulations and policies, enhance appeal and grievance procedures, and curtail illegal marketing practices. Additionally, CMS expects this rule to clarify timeframes and notification requirements.

Agency	Title of Rule (RIN)	Date Published	Cost-Benefit Analysis Information Provided in GAO Report
Department of Defense, Office of the Secretary	Retroactive Stop Loss Special Pay Compensation (0790-AI59)	4/16/2010	DoD did not include a cost-benefit analysis with the final rule. [In the preamble to the rule, DOD indicated that it was economically significant because "The Supplemental Appropriations Act, 2009 appropriated $534,400,000 to the Department of Defense, to remain available for obligation until expended: Provided, that such funds shall be available to the Secretaries of the military departments only to make payment of claims specified by this law."]
Department of Energy	Energy Conservation Program: Energy Conservation Standards for Residential Water Heaters, Direct Heating Equipment, and Pool Heaters (1904-AA90)	4/16/2010	DOE prepared a cost-benefit analysis in conjunction with the final rule. DOE determined that the standards adopted in the final rule will save approximately 2.81 quads Btu of energy over a 30-year period, and eliminate the need for approximately three new 250 MW power plants. The energy savings were estimated to result in cumulative greenhouse gas emission reductions of approximately 164 million tons of carbon dioxide, and alleviate air pollution by resulting in cumulative emissions reductions of approximately 124 kilotons of nitrogen oxides and 0.54 tons of power plant mercury. DOE determined that the annualized monetized benefits of the rule would be $1,676 million per year, using a 7-percent discount rate, and $2,020.5 million per year using a 3-percent discount rate. The costs are estimated to be $1,284.9 per year using a 7-percent discount rate, and $1,249.3 per year using a 3-percent discount rate.

Table A-1. (Continued)

Agency	Title of Rule (RIN)	Date Published	Cost-Benefit Analysis Information Provided in GAO Report
Department of Health and Human Services, Centers for Medicare & Medicaid Services	Medicaid Program; Final FY2008, Revised Preliminary FY2009, and Preliminary FY2010 Disproportionate Share Hospital Allotments and Final FY2008, Revised Preliminary FY2009, and Preliminary FY2010 Disproportionate Share Hospital Institutions for Mental Disease Limits (0938-AP66)	4/23/2010	CMS states that there are no changes between the preliminary and final FY2008 disproportionate share hospital (DSH) allotments and FY2008 IMD DSH limits because FY2008 was not determined to be the fiscal year specified for any state. CMS states that the revised preliminary FY2009 DSH allotments published in this notice are about $308 million greater than the preliminary FY2009 DSH allotments published in the Federal Register correction notice on January 26, 2009. 74 Fed. Reg. 4439. CMS states that this occurred because of the application of a higher CPI–U (4.4 percent in the revised preliminary determination compared to 4.0 percent in the original preliminary determination) and the application of the Recovery Act increase to states' DSH allotments for FY2009. The revised preliminary FY2009 IMD DSH limits being published in this notice are about $22 million greater than the preliminary FY2009 IMD DSH limits published in the Federal Register notice on December 19, 2008.

Agency	Title of Rule (RIN)	Date Published	Cost-Benefit Analysis Information Provided in GAO Report
Department of Health and Human Services, Centers for Medicare & Medicaid Services			73 Fed. Reg. 77,704. CMS notes that this is because the DSH allotment for a fiscal year is a factor in the determination of the IMD DSH limit for the fiscal year, and since the original preliminary FY2009 DSH allotments were increased in the revised preliminary FY2009 DSH allotments, the IMD DSH limits for some states were also increased. Additionally, CMS states that the preliminary FY2010 DSH allotments being published in this notice are about $277 million greater than the revised preliminary FY2009 DSH allotments being published in this notice and about $585 million greater than the preliminary FY2009 DSH allotments published in the Federal Register correction notice on January 26, 2009. 74 Fed. Reg. 4439. CMS explains that these increases are a direct result of the application of the Recovery Act provisions which in this case resulted in the FY2010 DSH allotments being determined as 2.5 percent greater than the FY2009 DSH allotments as determined under the Recovery Act.

Table A-1. (Continued)

Agency	Title of Rule (RIN)	Date Published	Cost-Benefit Analysis Information Provided in GAO Report
Department of Health and Human Services, Centers for Medicare & Medicaid Services			CMS states that the preliminary FY2010 IMD DSH limits being published in this notice are about $21 million greater than the revised preliminary FY2009 IMD DSH limits being published in this notice, and about $43 million greater than the preliminary FY2009 IMD DSH limits published in the Federal Register notice on December 19, 2008. 73 Fed. Reg. 77,704. CMS explains that this is because the DSH allotment for a fiscal year is a factor in the determination of the IMD DSH limit for the fiscal year, and since the preliminary FY2010 DSH allotments were increased as compared to the preliminary FY2009 DSH allotments, the associated FY2010 IMD DSH limits for some states were also increased.
Department of Health and Human Services, Centers for Medicare & Medicaid Services	Medicaid Program; State Flexibility for Medicaid Benefit Packages (0938-AP72)	4/30/2010	CMS states that the estimated aggregate federal savings for fiscal years 2006 through 2014 is $4.97 billion. CMS also states that the estimated aggregate state savings for fiscal years 2006 through 2014 is $3.36 billion. In the December 3, 2008, rule, CMS estimated aggregate impacts for fiscal years 2006 through 2010 of $2.28 billion in federal savings and $1.72 billion in state savings. In this final rule, the updated aggregate impacts, for the same time period of fiscal years 2006 through 2010, are $1.84 billion in federal savings and $1.05 billion in state savings.

Agency	Title of Rule (RIN)	Date Published	Cost-Benefit Analysis Information Provided in GAO Report
Department of Health and Human Services, Centers for Medicare & Medicaid Services			As a result, relative to the December 3, 2008, final rule, CMS notes that this yields a reduction in the aggregate impacts of $440 million in federal savings and $670 million in state savings, for fiscal years 2006 through 2010. CMS estimated the impact of this rule by analyzing the potential federal savings related to lower per capita spending that may be achieved if states choose to enroll beneficiaries in eligible populations in plans that are less costly than projected Medicaid costs.
Department of Health and Human Services, Centers for Medicare & Medicaid Services	Medicare Program; Inpatient Psychiatric Facilities Prospective Payment System Payment—Update for Rate Year Beginning July 1, 2010 (RY 2011) (0938-AP83)	4/30/2010	The net effect of the updates described in this notice results in an overall estimated $95 million increase in payments from rate year 2010 to rate year 2011. CMS does not expect changes in the quality of care or access to services for Medicare beneficiaries due to this notice. CMS contends that access to inpatient psychiatric facility (IPF) services will be enhanced due to the patient- and facility-level adjustment factors, all of which are intended to adequately reimburse IPFs for expensive cases. Also, the outlier policy is intended to assist IPFs that experience high-cost cases.
Department of the Treasury, Office of Thrift Supervision	Unfair or Deceptive Acts or Practices; Amendment (1550- AC38)	5/4/2010	In its current submission to the Comptroller General, OTS did not include any analysis of the final regulations. [In the preamble, OTS indicated that this rule removed a requirement that had been established by an earlier rule, which had been estimated to cost more than $100 million.]

Table A-1. (Continued)

Agency	Title of Rule (RIN)	Date Published	Cost-Benefit Analysis Information Provided in GAO Report
Department of Health and Human Services, Office of the Secretary	Early Retiree Reinsurance Program (0991-AB64)	5/5/2010	The Department of Health and Human Services (HHS) analyzed the costs and benefits of this interim final rule. HHS believes that the costs imposed on sponsors that want to receive the early retiree reimbursement will not be significant relative to the payments received. The costs will consist of staff or contractor time to complete the applications to participate, file claims for reimbursement, and to comply with program requirements such as requests related to an audit. HHS determined that this interim final rule contains information collection requirements under the Act. These information collection requirements are covered by the Office of Management and Budget (OMB) Control Number 0938-1087. HHS estimates that 11,300 respondents will generate 45,800 responses for a total burden of 854,675 hours and a total cost of $39,820,607. [In the preamble, HHS stated that "Congress appropriated funding of $5 billion for the temporary program," which "provides reimbursement to participating employment-based plans for a portion of the cost of health benefits for early retirees and their spouses, surviving spouses and dependents."]

Agency	Title of Rule (RIN)	Date Published	Cost-Benefit Analysis Information Provided in GAO Report
Environmental Protection Agency	Amendment to the Opt-Out and Recordkeeping Provisions in the Renovation, Repair, and Painting Program (2070-AJ55)	5/6/2010	EPA performed a cost-benefit analysis in conjunction with the final rule. The benefits of the final rule result from the prevention of adverse health affects attributable to lead exposure from renovations in pre-1978 buildings. The adverse health affects include impaired cognitive function in children and several illnesses in children and adults, such as increased cardiovascular outcomes (including increased blood pressure, increased incidence of hypertension, cardiovascular morbidity, and mortality) and decreased kidney function. EPA determined that annualized benefits from the final rule may range from approximately $870 million to $3.2 billion assuming a discount rate of 3 percent, and $920 million to $3.3 billion assuming a discount rate of 7 percent. The costs of the final rule result from removing the opt-out provision and requiring firms performing renovation, repair, and painting work for compensation in housing previously eligible for the opt-out provision to follow the training, certification, and work practice requirements of the Lead Renovation, Repair, and Painting (RRP) rule. In addition, the final rule adds recordkeeping requirements that will increase costs of renovations in all target housing and childoccupied facilities.

Table A-1. (Continued)

Agency	Title of Rule (RIN)	Date Published	Cost-Benefit Analysis Information Provided in GAO Report
Environmental Protection Agency			EPA estimates that the final rule will cost approximately $500 million in the first year, with the cost expected to drop to approximately $300 million per year starting with the second year, when improved test kits for detecting the presence of lead-based paint are assumed to become available. Training for renovators and workers and certification for firms working in housing previously covered by the opt-out provision is estimated to add approximately $50 million per year to the cost, and requiring renovators to provide owners and occupants with copies of the recordkeeping required to document compliance with the RRP rule training and work practice requirements costs approximately $30 million per year, with about two-thirds incurred in housing that was previously eligible for the opt-out provision.
Environmental Protection Agency and Department of Transportation, National Highway Traffic Safety Administration	Light-Duty Vehicle Greenhouse Gas Emission Standards and Corporate Average Fuel Economy Standards; Final Rule (2060-AP58; 2127-AK50)	5/7/2010	The agencies summarized the projected costs and benefits of the CAFE and GHG emissions standards. The agencies note that for several reasons, the estimates for costs and benefits presented by NHTSA and EPA, while consistent, are not directly comparable, and thus should not be expected to be identical.

Agency	Title of Rule (RIN)	Date Published	Cost-Benefit Analysis Information Provided in GAO Report
Environmental Protection Agency and Department of Transportation, National Highway Traffic Safety Administration			The agencies also state that it is important to note that there is significant overlap in costs and benefits for NHTSA's CAFE program and EPA's GHG program and therefore combined program costs and benefits, which together comprise the National Program, are not a sum of the two individual programs. Notably, NHTSA estimates that the total benefits of these CAFE standards will be more than three times the magnitude of the corresponding costs. NHTSA has analyzed in detail the costs and benefits of the final CAFE standards. NHTSA estimates that these new CAFE standards will lead to fuel savings totaling 61 billion gallons throughout the useful lives of vehicles sold in model years (MYs) 2012–2016. NHTSA states that at a 3-percent discount rate, the present value of the economic benefits resulting from those fuel savings is $143 billion and $112 billion at a 7-percent discount rate. NHTSA further estimates that these new CAFE standards will lead to corresponding reductions in CO2 emissions totaling 655 million metric tons during the useful lives of vehicles sold in MYs 2012–2016. Additionally, NHTSA estimates that the increases in technology application necessary to achieve the projected improvements in fuel economy will entail considerable monetary outlays.

Table A-1. (Continued)

Agency	Title of Rule (RIN)	Date Published	Cost-Benefit Analysis Information Provided in GAO Report
Environmental Protection Agency and Department of Transportation, National Highway Traffic Safety Administration			NHTSA estimates that incremental costs for achieving its standards—that is, outlays by vehicle manufacturers over and above those required to comply with the MY2011 CAFE standards—will total about $52 billion (i.e., during MYs 2012–2016). NHTSA projects that manufacturers will recover most or all of these additional costs through higher selling prices for new cars and light trucks. To allow manufacturers to recover these increased outlays (and, to a much lesser extent, the civil penalties that some companies are expected to pay for noncompliance), NHTSA estimates that the standards would lead to increases in average new vehicle prices ranging from $457 per vehicle in MY2012 to $985 per vehicle in MY2016. NHTSA concludes that its standards would produce net benefits of $130.7 billion at a 3-percent discount rate (with FFV credits, $138.2 billion) or $94.5 billion at a 7-percent discount rate over the useful lives of vehicles sold during MYs 2012–2016. EPA analyzed in detail the costs and benefits of the final GHG standards. Overall, EPA estimates that these new GHG standards for MY2012-2016 will lead to a combined fuel savings for light trucks and cars of 77.7 billion gallons of fuel.

Agency	Title of Rule (RIN)	Date Published	Cost-Benefit Analysis Information Provided in GAO Report
Environmental Protection Agency and Department of Transportation, National Highway Traffic Safety Administration			EPA states that at a 3- percent discount rate, the present value of the economic benefits resulting from those fuel savings is $182 billion and $142 billion at a 7-percent discount rate. The agency further estimates that these new GHG standards will lead to corresponding reductions in CO_2 emissions totaling 962 metric tons. EPA's estimated incremental and total technology outlays for cars and trucks for each of the model years 2012–2016 will total about $52 billion. EPA notes the technology outlays are for the industry as a whole and do not account for fuel savings associated with the program. EPA estimated the incremental cost increase of the average new vehicle for each model year 2012–2016. EPA explains that the values are incremental to a baseline vehicle and are not cumulative—in other words, the estimated increase for 2012 model year cars is $342 relative to a 2012 model year car absent the National Program, while the estimated increase for a 2013 model year car is $507 relative to a 2013 model year car absent the National Program (not $342 plus $507).

Table A-1. (Continued)

Agency	Title of Rule (RIN)	Date Published	Cost-Benefit Analysis Information Provided in GAO Report
Department of the Treasury, Internal Revenue Service; Department of Labor, Employee Benefits Security Administration; Department of Health and Human Services, Office of the Secretary	Interim Final Rules for Group Health Plans and Health Insurance Issuers Relating to Dependent Coverage of Children to Age 26 Under the Patient Protection and Affordable Care Act (1545- BJ46; 1210-AB41; 0991-AB66)	5/13/2010	The Department of the Treasury, Internal Revenue Service (IRS); Department of Labor, Employee Benefits Security Administration (EBSA); and Department of Health and Human Services, Office of the Secretary (HHS) (collectively, the agencies) analyzed the costs and benefits of these interim final rules. The agencies determined that the benefits are expected to outweigh the costs to the regulated community. For 2011, the agencies estimated the number of previously uninsured individuals who will be covered under their parents' coverage. The agencies estimated that under their low-range assumptions, 190,000 such individuals would be covered; under their mid-range assumptions, 650,000 such individuals; and under their high-range assumptions, 1.64 million such individuals. According to the agencies, expanding coverage options for the 19–25 population should decrease the number uninsured, which in turn should decrease the cost-shifting of uncompensated care onto those with coverage, increase the receipt of preventive health care, and provide more timely access to high quality care, resulting in a healthier population. In particular, the agencies predict children with chronic conditions or other serious health issues will be able to continue coverage through a parents' plan until age 26.

Agency	Title of Rule (RIN)	Date Published	Cost-Benefit Analysis Information Provided in GAO Report
Department of the Treasury, Internal Revenue Service; Department of Labor, Employee Benefits Security Administration; Department of Health and Human Services, Office of the Secretary			The agencies also expect that allowing extended dependent coverage will permit greater job mobility for this population as their health coverage will no longer be tied to their own jobs or student status. The agencies estimated the annual monetized costs of these interim final rules for 2011 through 2013 to be $11.2 million at a discount rate of 7 percent and $10.4 million at a discount rate of 3 percent.
Department of Education	Teacher Incentive Fund (1810- AB08)	5/21/2010	Education believes that the final priorities, requirements, definitions, and selection criteria outweigh any associated costs. Education believes that the costs imposed on applicants by the final rule will be limited to the paperwork burden related to preparing an application. The benefits of the final rule were expected to be the selection of high-quality applications to implement activities that are most likely to improve the quality of teaching and educational administration. The final rule was expected to result in an annualized monetary transfer of $437 million from the federal government to states, local educational agencies, and nonprofits.

Table A-1. (Continued)

Agency	Title of Rule (RIN)	Date Published	Cost-Benefit Analysis Information Provided in GAO Report
Department of Transportation, Federal Aviation Administration	Automatic Dependent Surveillance—Broadcast (ADSB) Out Performance Requirements To Support Air Traffic Control (ATC) Service (2120-AI92)	5/28/2010	FAA performed a cost-benefit analysis in conjunction with the final rule. FAA determined that the benefits of the final rule include the dollar savings in fuel, time, net reduction in CO2 emissions, and the consumer surplus associated with the additional flights accommodated because of the rule. FAA estimated that the quantified benefits of the final rule range from \$6.8 billion (\$2.1 billion at 7 percent present value) to \$8.5 billion (\$2.7 billion at 7 percent present value). FAA determined that the estimated incremental costs of the final rule range from a low of \$3.3 billion (\$2.2 billion at 7 percent present value) to a high of \$7.0 billion (\$4.1 billion at 7 percent present value). The costs include costs to the government, as well as to the aviation industry and other users of the National Airspace System (NAS), to deploy ADS-B, and are incremental to maintaining surveillance via current technology (radar). The aviation industry would begin incurring costs for avionics equipage in 2012 and would incur total costs ranging from \$2.5 billion (\$1.4 billion at 7 percent present value) to \$6.2 billion (\$3.3 billion at 7 percent present value) with an estimated midpoint of \$4.4 billion (\$2.3 billion at 7 percent present value) from 2012 to 2035.

Agency	Title of Rule (RIN)	Date Published	Cost-Benefit Analysis Information Provided in GAO Report
Department of Health and Human Services, Centers for Medicare & Medicaid Services	Medicare Program; Hospital Inpatient Prospective Payment Systems for Acute Care Hospitals and Fiscal Year 2010 Rates and to the Long-Term Care Hospital Prospective Payment System and Rate Year 2010 Rates: Final Fiscal Year 2010 Wage Indices and Payment Rates Implementing the Affordable Care Act (0938- AQ03)	6/2/2010	CMS conducted a cost-benefit analysis of this notice. CMS estimates that the operating payments to the IPPS will increase by approximately $75.7 million in FY2010; the capital payments will increase by approximately $94.7 million in FY2010. CMS estimates that payments to the LTCHs will decrease by approximately $11 million in FY2010. Both of these estimates reflect changes from the previously published estimates for FY2010.
Department of Agriculture, Commodity Credit Corporation	Conservation Stewardship Program (0578-AA43)	6/3/2010	CCC prepared a cost-effectiveness analysis (CEA) of the final rule, which is an approach used when benefits are not well understood or difficult to measure, but activity costs are available. The CEA compares the impact of these conservation activities in generating environmental benefits with program costs. The CEA describes how the improvements can produce beneficial impacts concerning onsite resource conditions, such as conserving soil, and significant offsite benefits, such as cleaner water, improved air quality, and enhanced wildlife habitat.

Table A-1. (Continued)

Agency	Title of Rule (RIN)	Date Published	Cost-Benefit Analysis Information Provided in GAO Report
Department of Agriculture, Commodity Credit Corporation			The total cumulative program costs for four program ranking periods are estimated to be $2.990 billion in constant 2005 dollars, discounted at 7 percent, or $3.520 billion in constant 2005 dollars discounted at 3 percent. Since the Conservation Stewardship Program is a voluntary program, it is not expected to impose any obligation or burden upon agricultural producers and non-industrial private forestland owners who chose not to participate.
Environmental Protection Agency	Prevention of Significant Deterioration and Title V Greenhouse Gas Tailoring Rule (2060-AP86)	6/3/2010	EPA examined the economic impacts of the final rule including the expected benefits and costs for affected sources and permitting authorities. EPA believes that this final rulemaking does not impose economic burdens or costs on any sources or permitting authorities, but should be viewed as regulatory relief for smaller GHG emission sources and for permitting authorities. According to EPA, there are no direct economic burdens or costs as a result of this final rule for larger sources of GHGs that will be required to obtain title V permits and/or comply on PSD requirements. EPA states that although larger sources will become subject to permitting on January 2, 2011, those impacts are not attributable to the present rulemaking because they are mandated by the CAA and existing regulations and automatically take effect independent of this action.

Agency	Title of Rule (RIN)	Date Published	Cost-Benefit Analysis Information Provided in GAO Report
Environmental Protection Agency			EPA also examined the social costs which will impose costs to society in the form of foregone environmental benefits resulting from GHG emission reductions that, absent this rule, might otherwise have occurred at sources deferred from permitting during the phase-in period. According to EPA, the net benefits of this GHG tailoring rule represent the difference between the benefits and costs of this rule to society. EPA states that the net benefits of the final rule for Steps 1 and 2 are \$193,598+B–C million for the 2 and one half year period where B denotes the unquantified benefits and C the quantified costs of this final rule. EPA states that these unquantified benefits of this rule include the avoided PSD best available control technology (BACT) costs for new and modifying sources and relate to the foregone environment benefits or GHG emission reductions that might be possible during the 2.5 year Step 1 and 2 phase-in period. EPA notes that these estimates are subject to significant uncertainties. EPA states that all dollar estimates shown are based upon 2007 dollars.

Table A-1. (Continued)

Agency	Title of Rule (RIN)	Date Published	Cost-Benefit Analysis Information Provided in GAO Report
Federal Reserve System	Electronic Fund Transfers (Docket No. R-1343)	6/4/2010	In its current submission to the Comptroller General, the Board did not include an analysis of the final regulations. The Board analyzed the cost and benefits of the final regulations in the November 2009 publication. See 74. Fed. Reg. 59,033. [The *Federal Register* citation provided indicates that "[u]sing the Federal Reserve's method, the total estimated annual burden for all financial institutions subject to Regulation E, including Federal Reserve-supervised institutions, would be approximately 853,059 hours." Based upon this information, CRS concluded that the paperwork costs are under $100 million.]
Nuclear Regulatory Commission	Revision of Fee Schedules; Fee Recovery for FY2010 (3150- AI70)	6/16/2010	In its submission of this final rule, the Nuclear Regulatory Commission (NRC) indicated that an analysis of cost and benefits was not applicable with respect to this rule. NRC stated that the annual fees, to the maximum extent practicable, have a reasonable relationship to the cost of regulatory services provided by NRC and will be assessed to those licensees NRC, in its discretion, determines can fairly, equitably, and practicably contribute to their payment. [In the rule summary, NRC stated that "the NRC's required fee recovery amount for the FY2010 budget is approximately $912.2 million.

Agency	Title of Rule (RIN)	Date Published	Cost-Benefit Analysis Information Provided in GAO Report
Nuclear Regulatory Commission			After accounting for billing adjustments, the total amount to be billed as fees is approximately $911.1 million"]
Department of the Treasury, Internal Revenue Service; Department of Labor, Employee Benefits Security Administration; Department of Health and Human Services	Interim Final Rules for Group Health Plans and Health Insurance Coverage Relating to Status as a Grandfathered Health Plan Under the Patient Protection and Affordable Care Act (1545-BJ51; 1210-AB42; 0991-AB68)	6/17/2010	With an estimated 2.2 million grandfathered plans in 2011, EBSA and IRS estimate an hour burden of approximately 538,000 hours with equivalent costs of $30.7 million. The Departments have estimated this as a one-time cost incurred in 2011, because after the first year, the Departments anticipate that any future costs will be de minimis. Overall, for both the grandfathering notice and the recordkeeping requirement, the Departments expect there to be a total hour burden of 1.1 million hours and a cost burden of $291,000. With an estimated 98,000 grandfathered plans and 7,400 grandfathered individual insurance products in 2011, HHS estimates an hour burden of approximately 26,000 hours with equivalent costs of $1.5 million. HHS has estimated this as a one-time cost incurred in 2011, because after the first year, HHS assumes any future costs will be de minimis. Overall, for both the grandfathering notice and the recordkeeping requirement, HHS expects there to be a total hour burden of 53,000 hours and a cost burden of $318,000.

Table A-1. (Continued)

Agency	Title of Rule (RIN)	Date Published	Cost-Benefit Analysis Information Provided in GAO Report
Environmental Protection Agency	Primary National Ambient Air Quality Standard for Sulfur Dioxide (2060-AO48)	6/22/2010	EPA stated that the Clean Air Act and judicial decisions make clear that the economic and technical feasibility of attaining the national ambient standards cannot be considered in setting or revising NAAQS, although such factors may be considered in the development of state implementation plans to implement the standards. Consequently, although EPA performed a cost-benefit analysis of the final rule, EPA did not consider the analysis in developing this final rule. [In the preamble, EPA estimated the costs of the rule at between $260 million and $4.4 billion, and estimated the net benefits at between $240 million and $79 billion (all in 2006 dollars).]
Department of State	Schedule of Fees for Consular Services, Department of State and Overseas Embassies and Consulates (1400-AC58)	6/28/2010	The Department conducted a cost-benefit analysis of this interim final rule. The Department noted that it generally sets consular fees at an amount calculated to achieve recovery of the costs to the United States of providing the consular service, in a manner consistent with general user charge principles. The increased fees include, for example, an increase in the application fee for a passport book for an adult from $44 to $70, and an increase in the passport book security surcharge from $20 to $40 to cover the costs of increased border security.

Agency	Title of Rule (RIN)	Date Published	Cost-Benefit Analysis Information Provided in GAO Report
Department of State			[In the preamble to the rule, the Department estimated that passport book application fees would increase by about $138 million per year, and the passport book security charge fee would increase about $238 million per year. Other fees were also expected to increase, but not by more than $100 million.]
Department of the Treasury, Internal Revenue Service; Department of Labor, Employee Benefits Security Administration; and Department of Health and Human Services	Patient Protection and Affordable Care Act: Preexisting Condition Exclusions, Lifetime and Annual Limits, Rescissions, and Patient Protections (1545-BJ61; 1210- AB43; 0991-AB69)	6/28/2010	The Department of the Treasury, Internal Revenue Service (IRS); Department of Labor, Employee Benefits Security Administration (EBSA); and Department of Health and Human Services (HHS) (collectively, the agencies) analyzed the costs and benefits of these interim final rules. The agencies stated that they crafted these interim final rules in the most economically efficient manner possible. The agencies estimate that these interim final rules will have an annual monetized cost of $4.9 million from 2011 to 2013. The agencies expect these interim final rules will expand coverage for children with preexisting conditions and individuals who face rescissions, lifetime limits, and annual limits as a result of high health care costs.

Table A-1. (Continued)

Agency	Title of Rule (RIN)	Date Published	Cost-Benefit Analysis Information Provided in GAO Report
Department of the Treasury, Internal Revenue Service; Department of Labor, Employee Benefits Security Administration; and Department of Health and Human Services			The agencies expect these benefits to manifest in a number of ways including: (1) increasing access to health care, improving health outcomes, improving worker productivity, and reducing family financial strain and "job lock"; (2) promoting equity, in the sense that the benefits will be enjoyed by those who are especially vulnerable as a result of health problems and financial status; (3) building better, sustained patient-provider relationships through choice of physician, resulting in decreased malpractice claims and improved medication adherence and health promotion; and (4) reducing administrative and time burdens on both patients and physicians while improving health outcomes by allowing quicker access to medical services when necessary by removing referrals and prior authorizations for primary care, obstetrical and gynecological care, and emergency servi ces.
Federal Reserve System	Truth in Lending (Docket No. R-1384)	6/29/2010	According to the Federal Reserve System (Board) submission, the Board did not prepare an analysis of the costs and benefits with respect to this final rule. [In the preamble, FRS said that the rule "requires that penalty fees imposed by card issuers be reasonable and proportional to the violation of the account terms.

Agency	Title of Rule (RIN)	Date Published	Cost-Benefit Analysis Information Provided in GAO Report
Federal Reserve System			The final rule also requires credit card issuers to reevaluate at least every six months annual percentage rates increased on or after January 1, 2009. The final rule also requires that notices of rate increases for credit card accounts disclose the principal reasons for the increase."]
Securities and Exchange Commission	Political Contributions by Certain Investment Advisers (3235-AK39)	7/14/2010	The Commission evaluated the costs and benefits of the final rule. With regard to benefits, the Commission stated that, overall, the rule is intended to address "pay to play" relationships that interfere with the legitimate process by which advisers are chosen based on the merits rather than on their contributions to political officials. The Commission noted that the potential for fraud to invade the various, intertwined relationships created by "pay to play" arrangements is without question. In addition, by leveling the playing field among advisers competing for state and local government business, the Commission expects the final rule will help minimize or eliminate manipulation of the market for advisory services provided to state and local governments. With regard to costs, the Commission recognized that an adviser with government clients will incur costs to monitor contributions and to establish procedures to comply with the final rule. The initial and ongoing compliance costs imposed by the final rule will vary significantly among firms.

Table A-1. (Continued)

Agency	Title of Rule (RIN)	Date Published	Cost-Benefit Analysis Information Provided in GAO Report
Securities and Exchange Commission			The Commission estimates that to establish and implement adequate compliance procedures, the final rule would impose initial compliance costs of approximately $2,352 per smaller firm, $29,407 per medium firm, and $58,813 per larger firm. The Commission also estimates that the final rule would impose annual, ongoing compliance expenses of approximately $2,940 per smaller firm, $117,625 per medium firm, and $235,250 per larger firm. In addition, the Commission estimates that to comply with provisions of this rule, advisers will incur an aggregate cost of approximately $200,246 per year and the non-labor cost burden to be $20,080,000.
Department of Labor, Employee Benefits Security Administration	Reasonable Contract or Arrangement Under Section 408(b)(2)—Fee Disclosure (1210-AB08)	7/16/2010	The Employee Benefits Security Administration (EBSA) evaluated the costs and benefits of this interim final rule. EBSA believes that mandatory proactive disclosure will reduce sponsor information costs, discourage harmful conflicts of interest, and enhance service value and that additional benefits will flow from EBSA's enhanced ability to redress abuse. EBSA did not quantify the benefits of this rule, but is confident they more than justify the cost. EBSA estimates that the annual cost of this rule from 2011 to 2020 to be approximately $58.7 million at a 7-percent discount rate and $54.3 million at a 3-percent discount rate.

Agency	Title of Rule (RIN)	Date Published	Cost-Benefit Analysis Information Provided in GAO Report
Department of Labor, Employee Benefits Security Administration			EBSA acknowledges in the rule that its estimates of the effects of the rule are, however, subject to some uncertainty.
Department of the Treasury, Internal Revenue Service; Department of Labor, Employee Benefits Security Administration; and Department of Health and Human Services	Interim Final Rules for Group Health Plans and Health Insurance Issuers Relating to Coverage of Preventive Services Under the Patient Protection and Affordable Care Act (1545-BJ60; 1210-AB44; 0938-AQ07)	7/19/2010	The agencies analyzed the potential costs and benefits of these interim final regulations. The agencies anticipate the qualitative costs from 2011 to 2013 to include new costs to the health care system resulting when beneficiaries increase their use of preventive services in response to the changes in coverage and cost-sharing requirements of preventive services. The agencies note that the magnitude of this effect on utilization depends on the price elasticity of demand and the percentage change in prices facing those with reduced cost sharing or newly gaining coverage. The agencies anticipate four qualitative benefits from 2011 to 2013. First, individuals will experience improved health as a result of reduced transmission, prevention or delayed onset, and earlier treatment of disease. Second, healthier workers and children will be more productive with fewer missed days of work or school. Third, some of the recommended preventive services will result in savings due to lower health care costs. Fourth, the cost of preventive services will be distributed more equitably.

Table A-1. (Continued)

Agency	Title of Rule (RIN)	Date Published	Cost-Benefit Analysis Information Provided in GAO Report
Department of Health and Human Services, Centers for Medicare & Medicaid Services	Medicare Program; Hospice Wage Index for Fiscal Year 2011 (0938-AP84)	7/22/2010	CMS estimates that the total hospice payments will increase by $220 million in FY2010 when both the 2.6 percent hospital market basket update and the 25 percent reduction in the BNAF and updated wage data are taken into account.
Department of Health and Human Services, Centers for Medicare & Medicaid Services	Medicare Program; Prospective Payment System and Consolidated Billing for Skilled Nursing Facilities for Fiscal Year 2011 (0938-AP87)	7/22/2010	The Centers for Medicare & Medicaid Services (CMS) analyzed the costs and benefits of this notice. CMS estimates that overall payments for skilled nursing facilities will increase by $542 million, or 1.7 percent, in fiscal year 2011 as compared to fiscal year 2010.
Department of Health and Human Services, Centers for Medicare & Medicaid Services	Medicare Program; Inpatient Rehabilitation Facility Prospective Payment System for Federal Fiscal Year 2011 (0938-AP89)	7/22/2010	CMS prepared a cost-benefit analysis for this notice and estimates that the total impact of these charges for fiscal year 2011 will be a net increase of $135 million in payments to IRF providers. Overall, the estimated payments per discharge for IRFs in fiscal year 2011 are projected to increase by 2.16 percent, compared with revised estimated payments in fiscal year 2010. IRF payments per discharge are estimated to increase 2.17 percent in urban areas, and 2.05 percent in rural areas, compared with the revised estimated fiscal year 2010 payments.

Agency	Title of Rule (RIN)	Date Published	Cost-Benefit Analysis Information Provided in GAO Report
Department of the Treasury, Internal Revenue Service; Department of Labor, Employee Benefits Security Administration; and Department of Health and Human Services	Interim Final Rules for Group Health Plans and Health Insurance Issuers Relating to Internal Claims and Appeals and External Review Processes Under the Patient Protection and Affordable Care Act (1545-BJ63; 1210-AB45; 0991-AB70)	7/23/2010	The Internal Revenue Service (IRS), the Employee Benefits Security Administration (EBSA), and the Department of Health and Human Services (HHS) (collectively, the agencies) analyzed the costs and benefits of this final rule. In assessing the benefits of this rule, the agencies found the following: "A more uniform, rigorous, and consumer friendly system of claims and appeals processing will provide a broad range of direct and indirect benefits that will accrue to varying degrees to all of the affected parties. These interim final regulations could improve the extent to which employee benefit plans provide benefits consistent with the established terms of individual plans. While payment of these benefits will largely constitute transfers, the transfers will be welfare improving, because incorrectly denied benefits will be paid. Greater certainty and consistency in the handling of benefit claims and appeals and improved access to information about the manner in which claims and appeals are adjudicated should lead to efficiency gains in the system, both in terms of the allocation of spending across plans and enrollees as well as operational efficiencies among individual plans. This certainty and consistency can also be expected to benefit, to varying degrees, all parties within the system, particularly consumers, and to lead to broader social welfare gains."

Table A-1. (Continued)

Agency	Title of Rule (RIN)	Date Published	Cost-Benefit Analysis Information Provided in GAO Report
Department of the Treasury, Internal Revenue Service; Department of Labor, Employee Benefits Security Administration; and Department of Health and Human Services			The agencies estimated the costs of this rule to (1) administer and conduct the internal and external review process, (2) prepare and distribute required disclosures and notices, and (3) bring plan and issuers' internal and external claims and appeals procedures into compliance with the new requirements. The agencies estimate these costs to be between $51.2 million and $51.6 million per year for the period 2011 to 2013, depending on the discount rate. The agencies also estimated the dollar amount of claim denials reversed in the external review process. While this amount is a cost to plans, it represents a payment of benefits that should have previously been paid to participants, but was denied. Part of this amount is a transfer from plans and issuers to those now receiving payment for denied benefits. These transfers will improve equity, because incorrectly denied benefits will be paid. Part of the amount could also be a cost if the reversal leads to services and hence resources being utilized now that had been denied previously. The agencies estimated the amount attributable to reversals to be between $24.4 million and $24.7 million per year for the period 2011 to 2013, depending on the discount rate. The agencies stated that they crafted the rules to secure the protections intended by Congress in the most economically efficient manner possible.

Agency	Title of Rule (RIN)	Date Published	Cost-Benefit Analysis Information Provided in GAO Report
Department of Agriculture, Commodity Credit Corporation	Conservation Reserve Program (0560-AH80)	7/28/2010	CCC states that the changes to CRP in this rule are expected to cost about $6.7 million per year over 10 years (2011–2020). CCC explains that this is a net cost that reflects roughly $77 million in additional CRP payments to participants over the next 10 years for additional land enrolled through the county maximum acreage waivers to exclude certain acreage and revised cropping history requirements and payments for pollinator habitat practices, minus roughly $10 million in reduced payments for the revised permissive uses. CCC states that the benefits to participants will be the net additional $6.7 million per year over the next 10 years. CCC notes that there are expected to be additional non-quantifiable environmental benefits from the waivers to exclude that will allow more environmentally sensitive acres to be enrolled through continuous signup, from additional highly erodible land enrollment that could result from making land in long-term hay rotations eligible, and from the incentives for pollinator habitat. Additionally, CCC states that the other provisions in this rule, such as local preference, are expected to have little to no cost. CCC believes that these provisions will largely substitute one CRP participant for another, or one practice for another, leading in a shift in costs and benefits to different participants and practices, but little net cost or benefit for CRP as a whole.

Table A-1. (Continued)

Agency	Title of Rule (RIN)	Date Published	Cost-Benefit Analysis Information Provided in GAO Report
Department of Health and Human Services, Centers for Medicare & Medicaid Services	Medicare and Medicaid Programs; Electronic Health Record Incentive Program (0938-AP78)	7/28/2010	The Centers for Medicare & Medicaid Services (CMS) analyzed the costs and benefits of this final rule. CMS estimates that the total cost to the Medicare and Medicaid programs will be $9.7 billion in transfers under a low scenario, and $27.4 billion under a high scenario, over a 10-year timeframe. In its analysis, CMS assumes that benefits to the program would accrue in the form of savings to Medicare, through the Medicare eligible professional payment adjustments. At this time, CMS is unable to quantify the expected qualitative benefits. However, CMS did identify benefits for eligible hospitals and professionals including reductions in medical recordkeeping costs, reductions in repeat tests, decreases in the length of stays, and reduced errors. CMS also identified benefits to society, including improved quality of care, better health outcomes, and more efficient delivery of health care.
Department of the Treasury, Office of the Comptroller of the Currency	Registration of Mortgage Loan Originators (1557-AD23)	7/28/2010	OCC performed a cost-benefit analysis of the final rule. OCC determined that, given the constraints imposed on OCC by the Secure and Fair Enforcement for Mortgage Licensing Act of 2008, and based on the estimated mean cost, the final rule was the least cost option available to OCC.

Agency	Title of Rule (RIN)	Date Published	Cost-Benefit Analysis Information Provided in GAO Report
Department of the Treasury, Office of the Comptroller of the Currency			[The preamble indicated that the rule required mortgage loan originators employed by national banks to register with the Nationwide Mortgage Licensing System and Registry and maintain their registration. Mortgage loan originators were also required to obtain a unique identifier through the registry that will remain with that originator, regardless of changes in employment. In addition, the rule required mortgage loan originators and national banks to provide these unique identifiers to consumers in certain circumstances, and requires national banks to adopt and follow written procedures to assure compliance with the registration requirements. Although the agencies indicated that these requirements would impose certain regulatory costs, they did not provide monetized estimates of those costs in the rule.]
Department of Health and Human Services	Pre-Existing Condition Insurance Plan Program (0991- AB71)	7/30/2010	The Department of Health and Human Services (HHS) analyzed the costs and benefits of this interim final rule. In assessing the benefits of this rule, HHS stated that the Pre-existing Condition Insurance Plan (PCIP) will provide uninsured Americans with pre-existing conditions and that have been denied coverage or otherwise excluded from purchasing insurance coverage an opportunity to obtain coverage.

Table A-1. (Continued)

Agency	Title of Rule (RIN)	Date Published	Cost-Benefit Analysis Information Provided in GAO Report
Department of Health and Human Services			HHS determined that providing this insurance option will increase access to health care and reduce financial strain for participants and will likely improve health outcomes and worker productivity. HHS found that individuals who are especially vulnerable as a result of existing health problems and financial status may receive the greatest benefit from this program. HHS estimated that the annual reporting and recordkeeping costs associated with this interim final rule will be $1,939,020. HHS determined that, to the extent PCIP increases access to health care services, increased health care utilization and costs will result due to increased uptake. HHS also identified administrative costs of the rule, including the cost of contractors to apply, the time cost for individuals to apply, and the contractors' costs of complying with program rules (e.g., conducting appeals, preventing fraud). Finally HHS estimates that under this rule $5 billion in federal funds will be transferred to contractors to aid in administering the program.

Agency	Title of Rule (RIN)	Date Published	Cost-Benefit Analysis Information Provided in GAO Report
Department of Homeland Security, U.S. Customs and Border Protection	Electronic System for Travel Authorization (ESTA): Travel Promotion Fee and Fee for Use of the System (1651-AA83)	8/9/2010	DHS conducted a cost-benefit analysis of this interim final rule. DHS concluded that the annualized cost to applicants, primarily in the form of transfers from foreign citizens to the U.S. government, is estimated between $152 million and $258 million. With respect to benefits, DHS states that this interim final rule allows DHS to comply with the Travel Promotion Act of 2009 (TPA), which was contained in section 9 of the United States Capitol Police Administrative Technical Corrections Act of 2009, P.L. 111- 145, and enhances security.
Department of Labor, Occupational Safety and Health Administration	Cranes and Derricks in Construction (1218-AC01)	8/9/2010	Occupational Safety and Health Administration (OSHA) analyzed the costs and benefits of this final rule. OSHA estimated that the annualized costs include the costs of crane assembly and disassembly ($16.3 million), power line safety ($68.2 million), crane inspections ($16.5 million), ground conditions ($2.3 million), and operator qualification and certification ($50.7 million) for a total annualized cost of $154.1 million. OSHA estimated that the annual benefits include injuries prevented (175), fatalities prevented (22), and property damage from tipovers prevented ($7 million) for total monetized benefits of $209.3 million.

Table A-1. (Continued)

Agency	Title of Rule (RIN)	Date Published	Cost-Benefit Analysis Information Provided in GAO Report
Department of Health and Human Services, Centers for Medicare & Medicaid Services	Medicare Program; End-Stage Renal Disease Prospective Payment System (0938-AP57)	8/12/2010	The Centers for Medicare & Medicaid Services (CMS) analyzed the costs and benefits of this final rule. CMS's analysis shows an overall decrease in payments to all end-stage renal disease facilities for renal dialysis of 2 percent, or approximately $200 million, from what the payments would have been in the absence of this rule in calendar year 2011.
Securities and Exchange Commission	Amendments to Form ADV (3235-AI17)	8/12/2010	The Commission conducted a cost-benefit analysis of this final rule. With respect to benefits, the Commission stated, in part, that the new narrative brochures and electronic filing provide substantial benefits to advisory clients and prospective clients. The brochures present clients with critically important information they need to determine whether to hire or continue the services of a particular adviser. This information will be presented in a uniform format easy for most investors to understand. In addition, investors searching for an adviser will be able to access the firm's brochures through the Commission's public disclosure Web site. With respect to costs, the Commission estimates that advisers would incur costs of approximately $33,639,960 in drafting the new brochures and supplements in the first year.

Agency	Title of Rule (RIN)	Date Published	Cost-Benefit Analysis Information Provided in GAO Report
Securities and Exchange Commission			Advisers may also incur costs of approximately $22,775,400 in connection with their use of outside legal services and compliance consulting services to assist in preparation of their Form ADV. The Commission also estimates that advisers would incur annual costs of $1,620,462. The Commission estimates annual delivery costs of $18,918,802.
Department of Health and Human Services, Centers for Medicare & Medicaid Services	Medicare Program; Hospital Inpatient Prospective Payment Systems for Acute Care Hospitals and the Long-Term Care Hospital Prospective Payment System Changes and FY2011 Rates; Provider Agreements and Supplier Approvals; and Hospital Conditions of Participation for Rehabilitation and Respiratory Care Services; Medicaid Program: Accreditation for Providers of Inpatient Psychiatric Services (0938- AP80; 0938-AP33)	8/16/2010	The Centers for Medicare & Medicaid Services (CMS) analyzed the costs and benefits of this final rule. CMS estimated that the final applicable percentage increase to the inpatient prospective payment systems (IPPS) rates required by the statute, in conjunction with other final payment changes in this final rule, will result in a $440 million decrease in fiscal year 2011 operating payments (or -0.4 percent decrease) and an estimated $21 million decrease in fiscal year 2011 capital payments (or -0.5 percent change). In addition, long-term care hospitals (LTCHs) are expected to experience an increase in payments by $22.3 million (or 0.5 percent).

Table A-1. (Continued)

Agency	Title of Rule (RIN)	Date Published	Cost-Benefit Analysis Information Provided in GAO Report
Federal Reserve System	Electronic Fund Transfers (Docket No. R-1377)	8/17/2010	In its submission to the Comptroller General, the Board did not include a cost-benefit analysis. [In the preamble, FRS stated that the rule implemented the recently enacted "Gift Card Amendment" (P.L. 111- 203), which provides a delayed effective date with respect to provisions the Credit Card Act (P.L. 111- 24) in order to permit the sale of existing card stock through January 31, 2011. Among other things, the delayed provisions would have imposed certain restrictions on a person's ability to impose dormancy, inactivity, or service fees with respect to gift certificates, store gift cards, and general-use prepaid cards.]
Environmental Protection Agency	National Emission Standards for Hazardous Air Pollutants for Reciprocating Internal Combustion Engines (2060- AP36)	8/20/2010	Based on estimated compliance costs on all sources associated with this final rule and the predicted change in prices and production in the affected industries assuming passthrough of costs to affected consumers, EPA believes the estimated social costs of this final rule are $253 million (2009 dollars). EPA states that the total monetized benefits of this final rule in 2013 range from $510 million to $1.2 billion (2009 dollars, 3 percent discount rate).

Agency	Title of Rule (RIN)	Date Published	Cost-Benefit Analysis Information Provided in GAO Report
Department of the Interior, Fish and Wildlife Service	Migratory Bird Hunting; Final Frameworks for Early-Season Migratory Bird Hunting Regulations (1018-AX06)	8/30/2010	Interior relied on the economic analysis that was prepared for the 2008-09 season, because it chose to issue identical regulations to past seasons for ducks, and made only minor modifications to the season frameworks for other species. According to Interior, the modifications will not significantly change the economic impacts of the rule which were not quantified for other species. Interior estimated a consumer surplus of $205-270 million.
Department of the Interior, Fish and Wildlife Service	Migratory Bird Hunting; Early Seasons and Bag and Possession Limits for Certain Migratory Game Birds in the Contiguous United States, Alaska, Hawaii, Puerto Rico, and the Virgin Islands (1018- AX06)	8/31/2010	Interior relied on the economic analysis that was prepared for the 2008-09 season, because it chose to issue identical regulations to past seasons for ducks, and made only minor modifications to the season frameworks for other species. According to Interior, the modifications will not significantly change the economic impacts of the rule which were not quantified for other species. Interior estimated a consumer surplus of $205-270 million.
Department of Veterans Affairs	Diseases Associated With Exposure to Certain Herbicide Agents (Hairy Cell Leukemia and Other Chronic B-Cell Leukemias, Parkinson's Disease and Ischemic Heart Disease) (2900-AN54)	8/31/2010	In the proposed rule, VA estimated the total cost for this rulemaking to be $13.6 billion during FY2010, $25.3 billion for 5 years, and $42.2 billion over 10 years. However, VA now knows that based on the publication date of the final rulemaking the timing will not allow payments to begin prior to FY2011. As a result, VA expects FY2010 and FY2011 costs will both now occur in FY2011.

Table A-1. (Continued)

Agency	Title of Rule (RIN)	Date Published	Cost-Benefit Analysis Information Provided in GAO Report
Department of Veterans Affairs			These costs include retroactive benefit costs in the first year and increased benefit costs for veterans currently on the rolls.
Department of the Interior, Fish and Wildlife Service	Migratory Bird Hunting; Migratory Bird Hunting Regulations on Certain Federal Indian Reservations and Ceded Lands for the 2010-11 Early Season	9/1/2010	Interior relied on the economic analysis that was prepared for the 2008-09 season, because it chose to issue identical regulations to past seasons for ducks, and made only minor modifications to the season frameworks for other species. According to Interior, the modifications will not significantly change the economic impacts of the rule which were not quantified for other species. Interior estimated a consumer surplus of $205-270 million.
Environmental Protection Agency	National Emission Standards for Hazardous Air Pollutants From the Portland Cement Manufacturing Industry and Standards of Performance for Portland Cement Plants (2060-AO15; 2060-AO42)	9/9/2010	EPA summarizes the total monetized benefits for the final NESHAP and NSPS amendments in the implementation year, 2013. EPA estimates that the total monetized benefits will be between $7.4 to $18 billion (2005 dollars), at a 3-percent discount rate and $6.7 to $16 billion (2005 dollars), at a 7-percent discount rate. EPA performed two separate cost analyses for this final rule, an engineering analysis and an Industrial Sector Integrated Solutions (ISIS) model. In the engineering analysis, EPA estimates the total capital cost of installing alkaline scrubbers and ACI systems for mercury control, including monitoring systems, will be $339 million with an annualized cost of $113 million.

Agency	Title of Rule (RIN)	Date Published	Cost-Benefit Analysis Information Provided in GAO Report
Environmental Protection Agency			EPA notes that where ACI does not provide sufficient control of organic hazardous air pollutants (HAP) and THC, RTO/wet scrubbers are used with an estimated capital cost of installation at $253 million with annualized cost of $49 million. EPA states that the capital cost of adding scrubbers for the control of HCl is estimated to be $1,882 million with an annualized cost of $261 million. EPA also states that the capital cost of adding membrane bags to existing fabric will be $57 million with annualized cost of $16 million. Additionally, EPA believes the total capital cost for the final amendments for kilns subject to existing source emissions limits will be an estimated $2.2 billion with an annualized cost of $377 million. EPA states that the estimated emission control capital cost per new 1.2 million tons per year (tpy) kiln is $3.2 million and the annualized costs are estimated at $1.2 million for mercury and THC/organic HAP control, and $3.6 million for HCl control. According to EPA, because the new kiln will be equipped with a baghouse even in the absence of the rule and because the ACI system, which includes a polishing baghouse, will be installed for mercury and organic HAP control, there will be no additional cost for PM control.

Table A-1. (Continued)

Agency	Title of Rule (RIN)	Date Published	Cost-Benefit Analysis Information Provided in GAO Report
Environmental Protection Agency			EPA notes that under the NSPS, 7 new kilns will install SNCR to control NOX and add NOX CEMS at a capital cost of $19.6 million and an annualized cost of $10.9 million. EPA believes that the control of SO2 under the NSPS will be accomplished by wet scrubbers installed for HCl control under the NESHAP so that no control costs are attributable to the NSPS. EPA states that there will be SO2 monitoring cost estimated at $1.1 million capital cost and $0.3 million annualized cost for the 7 new kilns subject to the NSPS. EPA notes that flow monitoring devices are needed in conjunction with CEMS for NOX and SO2. Additionally, EPA states that capital costs for flow monitoring devices will be $0.25 million capital and $0.1 million annualized costs. According to EPA, national annualized cost by the end of the fifth year for all new kilns will be an estimated $80.6 million. In the ISIS results, EPA is not able to separate costs by pollutant because the model provides an overall optimization of the production and air pollution control costs. EPA notes that the total annual costs of the ISIS model for the NESHAP and NSPS are $350 million in 2013. EPA believes that this estimate is significantly lower than the total costs estimated by traditional methods.

Agency	Title of Rule (RIN)	Date Published	Cost-Benefit Analysis Information Provided in GAO Report
Department of Justice	Nondiscrimination on the Basis of Disability in State and Local Government Services (1190- AA46)	9/15/2010	The Department's final regulatory impact analysis (RIA), estimates the benefits and costs for all new (referred to as "supplemental") requirements and revised requirements across all types of newly constructed and existing facilities. The Department states that the final rules increase social resources and thus represent a public good because monetized benefits exceed monetized costs—that is, the regulations have a positive net present value (NPV). The Department notes that under every scenario assessed in the final RIA, the final rules have a positive NPV. According to the Department, the final RIA's first scenario examines the incremental impact of the final rules using the "main" set of assumptions (i.e., assuming a primary baseline (the original 1991 ADA Standards), that the safe harbor applies, and that for title III entities barrier removal is readily achievable for 50 percent of elements subject to supplemental requirements). Under this set of assumptions, the Department states that the final rules have an expected NPV of $9.3 billion (7 percent discount rate) and $40.4 billion (3 percent discount rate). Additionally, the Department states that the RIA recognizes that additional benefits are likely to result from the new standards. According to the Department, many of these benefits are more difficult to quantify.

Table A-1. (Continued)

Agency	Title of Rule (RIN)	Date Published	Cost-Benefit Analysis Information Provided in GAO Report
Department of Justice			The Department explains that among the potential benefits that have been discussed by researchers and advocates are reduced administrative costs due to harmonized guidelines, increased business opportunities, increased social development, and improved health benefits.
Department of Justice	Nondiscrimination on the Basis of Disability by Public Accommodations and in Commercial Facilities (1190-AA44)	9/15/2010	The Department's final regulatory impact analysis (RIA), estimates the benefits and costs for all new (referred to as "supplemental") requirements and revised requirements across all types of newly constructed and existing facilities. The Department states that the final rules increase social resources and thus represent a public good because monetized benefits exceed monetized costs—that is, the regulations have a positive net present value (NPV). The Department notes that under every scenario assessed in the final RIA, the final rules have a positive NPV. According to the Department, the final RIA's first scenario examines the incremental impact of the final rules using the "main" set of assumptions (i.e., assuming a primary baseline (the original 1991 ADA Standards), that the safe harbor applies, and that for title III entities barrier removal is readily achievable for 50 percent of elements subject to supplemental requirements).

Agency	Title of Rule (RIN)	Date Published	Cost-Benefit Analysis Information Provided in GAO Report
Department of Justice			Under this set of assumptions, the Department states that the final rules have an expected NPV of $9.3 billion (7 percent discount rate) and $40.4 billion (3 percent discount rate) Additionally, the Department states that the RIA recognizes that additional benefits are likely to result from the new standards. According to the Department, many of these benefits are more difficult to quantify. The Department explains that among the potential benefits that have been discussed by researchers and advocates are reduced administrative costs due to harmonized guidelines, increased business opportunities, increased social development, and improved health benefits.
Securities and Exchange Commission	Facilitating Shareholder Director Nominations (3235- AK27)	9/16/2010	SEC believes that Rule 14a–11 and the amendment to Rule 14a–8(i)(8), where applicable, will offer four benefits. First, SEC states that the final rule will facilitate shareholders' abilities to exercise their traditional state law rights to nominate and elect directors. Second, SEC notes that the final rule will establish a minimum uniform procedure pursuant to which shareholders will be able to include their director nominees in a company's proxy materials and enhance shareholders' abilities to propose alternative procedures that further shareholders' rights to nominate and elect directors. Third, SEC states that the final rule will potentially improve overall board and company performance.

Table A-1. (Continued)

Agency	Title of Rule (RIN)	Date Published	Cost-Benefit Analysis Information Provided in GAO Report
Securities and Exchange Commission			Finally, SEC believes the final rule will result in more informed voting decisions in director elections due to improved disclosure of shareholder director nominations and enhanced communications between shareholders regarding director nominations. SEC anticipate that the new rules, where applicable, may result in costs related to potential adverse effects on company and board performance; additional complexity in the proxy process; and preparing the required disclosures, printing and mailing, and costs of additional solicitations. SEC also states that the new rules may result in additional costs. SEC explains that with respect to investment companies, one commenter stated that if a shareholder nomination causes an election to be "contested" under rules of the New York Stock Exchange, brokers would not be able to vote client shares on a discretionary basis, making it difficult and more expensive for investment companies to achieve a quorum for a meeting. SEC recognizes that it may be more costly for investment companies to achieve a quorum in such a situation, but believes, however, that the costs imposed on investment companies will be limited.

Agency	Title of Rule (RIN)	Date Published	Cost-Benefit Analysis Information Provided in GAO Report
Securities and Exchange Commission			SEC notes that its decision to adopt, as proposed, the revisions to Rule 14a–6(a)(4) and Note 3 to the rule means that the inclusion of a shareholder director nominee in the company's proxy materials will not require the company to file preliminary proxy materials, provided that the company was otherwise qualified to file directly in definitive form. SEC states that because the proxy materials will not be filed in preliminary form, SEC staff may not have the opportunity to review these proxy materials before companies make definitive copies available to shareholders. SEC believes staff review of preliminary materials can benefit shareholders by helping to assure that companies comply with the federal proxy rules and provide appropriate disclosure to shareholders. SEC believes, however, that any cost related to the staff's inability to review preliminary proxy materials is mitigated by the staff's ability to review the disclosure contained in the Schedule 14N as well as in any additional soliciting materials filed by either the company or the nominating shareholder or group. Further, SEC notes that it recently stated that the staff retains the right to comment on proxy materials filed in definitive form if the staff deems that to be appropriate under the circumstances.

Table A-1. (Continued)

Agency	Title of Rule (RIN)	Date Published	Cost-Benefit Analysis Information Provided in GAO Report
Department of the Interior, Fish and Wildlife Service	Migratory Bird Hunting; Final Frameworks for Late-Season Migratory Bird Hunting Regulations (1018-AX06)	9/23/2010	Interior relied on the economic analysis that was prepared for the 2008-09 season, because it chose to issue identical regulations to past seasons for ducks, and made only minor modifications to the season frameworks for other species. According to Interior, the modifications will not significantly change the economic impacts of the rule which were not quantified for other species. Interior estimated a consumer surplus of $205-270 million.
Department of Homeland Security	U.S. Citizenship and Immigration Services Fee Schedule (1615-AB80)	9/24/2010	The final rule will provide DHS with an average of $209 million in FY2010 and FY2011 annual fee revenue, based on a projected annual fee-paying volume of 4.4 million immigration benefit requests and 1.9 million requests for biometric services, over the fee revenue that would be collected under the current fee structure. The increased revenue will be used to fund the full cost of processing immigration benefit applications and associated support benefits; the full cost of providing similar benefits to asylum and refugee applicants; and the full cost of similar benefits provided to others at no charge.

Agency	Title of Rule (RIN)	Date Published	Cost-Benefit Analysis Information Provided in GAO Report
Department of the Interior, Fish and Wildlife Service	Migratory Bird Hunting; Late Seasons and Bag and Possession Limits for Certain Migratory Game Birds (1018- AX06)	9/24/2010	Interior relied on the economic analysis that was prepared for the 2008-09 season, because it chose to issue identical regulations to past seasons for ducks, and made only minor modifications to the season frameworks for other species. According to Interior, the modifications will not significantly change the economic impacts of the rule which were not quantified for other species. Interior estimated a consumer surplus of $205-270 million.
Department of the Interior, Fish and Wildlife Service	Migratory Bird Hunting; Migratory Bird Hunting Regulations on Certain Federal Indian Reservations and Ceded Lands for the 2010-11 Late Season (1018-AX06)	9/24/2010	Interior relied on the economic analysis that was prepared for the 2008-09 season, because it chose to issue identical regulations to past seasons for ducks, and made only minor modifications to the season frameworks for other species. According to Interior, the modifications will not significantly change the economic impacts of the rule which were not quantified for other species. Interior estimated a consumer surplus of $205-270 million.
Department of the Interior, Bureau of Ocean Energy Management, Regulation and Enforcement	Oil and Gas and Sulphur Operations in the Outer Continental Shelf—Increased Safety Measures for Energy Development on the Outer Continental Shelf (1010-AD68)	10/14/2010	BOEMRE states that the cost-benefit analysis for this rule was conducted using a scenario analysis. BOEMRE explains that the cost-benefit analysis considers a regulation designed to reduce the likelihood of a catastrophic oil spill, while the costs are the compliance costs of imposed regulation.

Table A-1. (Continued)

Agency	Title of Rule (RIN)	Date Published	Cost-Benefit Analysis Information Provided in GAO Report
Department of the Interior, Bureau of Ocean Energy Management, Regulation and Enforcement			BOEMRE notes that if another catastrophic oil spill is prevented, the benefits are the avoided costs associated with a catastrophic oil spill (e.g., reduction in expected natural resource damages owing to the reduction in likelihood of failure). Noting that the estimated costs of this rulemaking, as reflected in the compliance costs of the enumerated requirements of approximately $180 million per year, have a strong foundation and are based on surveys of public and industry sources, BOEMRE states that quantification of the benefits is uncertain. BOEMRE believes the benefits are represented by the avoided costs of a catastrophic spill, which are estimated under the stipulated scenario as being $16.3 billion per spill avoided. According to BOEMRE, these regulations will reduce the likelihood of another blowout and associated spill, but the risk reduction associated with the specific provisions of this rulemaking cannot be quantified because there are many complex factors that affect the risk of a blowout event.

Agency	Title of Rule (RIN)	Date Published	Cost-Benefit Analysis Information Provided in GAO Report
Department of Defense, Office of the Secretary	Civilian Health and Medical Program of the Uniformed Services (CHAMPUS)/TRICARE: Inclusion of TRICARE Retail Pharmacy Program in Federal Procurement of Pharmaceuticals (0720-AB45)	10/15/2010	DOD referenced a Government Accountability Office report, "DOD Pharmacy Program: Continued Efforts Needed to Reduce Growth in Spending at Retail Pharmacies," April 2008 (GAO–08–327), which found that DOD's drug spending "more than tripled from $1.6 billion in fiscal year 2000 to $6.2 billion in fiscal year 2006" and that retail pharmacy spending "drove most of this increase, rising almost nine-fold from $455 million to $3.9 billion and growing from 29 percent of overall drug spending to 63 percent." DOD concurs in these findings and notes that the principal economic impact of this final rule is to moderate somewhat the rate of growth in spending in the retail pharmacy component of the program. At various times since the enactment of NDAA–08, DOD estimated the reduced spending associated with applying FCPs to the Retail Pharmacy Network. DOD funds the Military Health System through two separate mechanisms. One is the Defense Health Program (DHP) appropriation, which pays for health care for all beneficiaries except those who are also eligible for Medicare. DOD-funded health care for DOD beneficiaries who are also eligible for Medicare is paid for by way of an accrual fund called the Medicare-Eligible Retiree Health Care Fund (MERHCF) under 10 U.S.C. chapter 56. Funds are paid into the MERHCF from military personnel appropriations and the general U.S. treasury.

Table A-1. (Continued)

Agency	Title of Rule (RIN)	Date Published	Cost-Benefit Analysis Information Provided in GAO Report
Department of Defense, Office of the Secretary			At the time of the 2008 proposed rule, for example, DOD estimated Fiscal Years (FY) 2010 reduced spending of $388 million for the DHP and $404 for the MERHCF. At the time of the 2009 final rule, DOD used a different estimating model and estimated much larger savings, including for FY–10 for example, reduced spending of $761 million for the DHP and $910 for the MERHCF. Based on experience since issuance of the final rule and a refined estimating model, DOD now estimates that the reduced spending will be closer to the original, lower estimates. DOD's current estimated cost reductions from applying FCPs to the TRICARE Retail Pharmacy Network in Fiscal Years 2010 through 2015 ranges from $375 million to $560 millon for DHP reduced spending and $474 million to $707 million for MERHCF reduced spending. FCP savings estimates will continue to be updated as actual refunds are received and estimating methodologies are refined. As a frame of reference, total TRICARE Pharmacy Benefits Program spending is estimated to be $8.5 billion in FY2010.

Agency	Title of Rule (RIN)	Date Published	Cost-Benefit Analysis Information Provided in GAO Report
Department of Labor, Employee Benefits Security Administration	Fiduciary Requirements for Disclosure in Participant- Directed Individual Account Plans (1210-AB07)	10/20/2010	The Department of Labor, Employee Benefits Security Administration (EBSA), analyzed the costs and benefits of this final rule and concluded that the benefits of the rule justify its costs. EBSA identified two primary benefits of this rule: (1) reduced time for plan participants to collect investment-related information and organize it into a format that allows the information to be compared and (2) improved investment results for plan participants due to the enhanced disclosures available to them. EBSA estimates that the present value of the benefits over the 10-year period 2012–2021 will be about $14.9 billion, with a low estimate of $7.2 billion and a high estimate of $29.9 billion. EBSA expects the costs of this final rule to include: (1) costs due to upfront review and updating of plan documents, (2) costs due to production of quarterly dollar amount disclosures, (3) costs due to assembling required information for chart and web site, (4) costs due to the web site requirement, (5) cost of distribution and materials for disclosures, and (6) discouragement of some employers from sponsoring a retirement plan. EBSA estimates that the present value of the costs over the 10-year period 2012–2021 will be $2.7 billion, with a low estimate of $2.0 billion and a high estimate of $3.3 billion.

Table A-1. (Continued)

Agency	Title of Rule (RIN)	Date Published	Cost-Benefit Analysis Information Provided in GAO Report
Department of Labor, Employee Benefits Security Administration			Overall, EBSA estimates that this final rule will generate a net present value (or net present benefit) of almost $12.3 billion.
Securities and Exchange Commission	Reporting of Security-Based Swap Transaction Data (3235- AK73)	10/20/2010	The Commission performed a preliminary cost-benefit analysis in conjunction with the interim final temporary rule and requested comments on the costs and benefits. The Commission determined that the interim final temporary rule will provide a means for the Commission to gain a better understanding of the security-based swap markets and help the Commission analyze the security-based swap market as a whole and identify risks. The interim final temporary rule will also facilitate the reports the Commission is required to provide to Congress on security-based swaps and the security-based swaps marketplace, along with having possible benefits in encouraging management review of internal procedures and controls by market participants. The Commission preliminarily estimates that the interim final temporary rule could affect more than 1,000 market participants and cover approximately 2.4 million security-based swap transactions.

Agency	Title of Rule (RIN)	Date Published	Cost-Benefit Analysis Information Provided in GAO Report
Securities and Exchange Commission			The Commission preliminarily estimates that amending internal procedures, reprogramming systems, and implementing compliance processes to ensure that pre-enactment security-based swap transaction data is preserved could result in a cost to each respondent of approximately $6,236 and an aggregate cost of approximately $6,236,000. The Commission preliminarily estimates that the requirement to report the transaction confirmation and time, if available, of execution could result in a cost to each reporting entity of approximately $43,900 and an aggregate cost of approximately $43,900,000. Finally, the Commission preliminarily estimates that responding to Commission requests for information and documents could result in a cost to each reporting entity of approximately $6,352 and an aggregate cost of approximately $6,352,000.
Department of Agriculture, Farm Service Agency	Crop Assistance Program (0560-AI11)	10/25/2010	The Farm Service Agency (FSA) analyzed the costs and benefits of this interim rule. FSA estimated that the total cost to the government, and the corresponding benefit to producers, for the Crop Assistance Program will be between $137 million and $543 million, depending on how many producers in disaster counties apply for payment.

Table A-1. (Continued)

Agency	Title of Rule (RIN)	Date Published	Cost-Benefit Analysis Information Provided in GAO Report
Department of Education	High School Equivalency Program and College Assistance Migrant Program, The Federal TRIO Programs, and Gaining Early Awareness and Readiness for Undergraduate Program (1840- AD01)	10/26/2010	Education determined that the potential costs associated with the final rule are those resulting from statutory requirements and those determined by Education as necessary for administering the program effectively and efficiently. Education determined that the benefits of the regulation, which include $1.233 billion in grant funds from the federal government to institutions of higher education, public and private agencies and organizations, and secondary schools, justify the costs.
Department of Agriculture	Commodity Credit Corporation: Biomass Crop Assistance Program (0560- AH92)	10/27/2010	USDA prepared a cost-benefit analysis in conjunction with the final rule. The total outlays are $461 million in constant (2011) dollars. Because the payments under the final rule are essentially transfer payments, the costs to the government equal the benefits to biomass crop assistance program (BCAP) producers and biomass crop farms.
Department of Education	Program Integrity Issues (1840- AD02)	10/29/2010	The Department of Education (Education) analyzed the costs and benefits of this final rule. Education identified benefits provided in these regulations, including: updated administrative procedures for federal student aid programs; a definition and process to determine the validity of a student's high school diploma; enhanced reliability and security of ability-to-benefit tests; an additional option for students to prove ability to benefit by successfully completing college coursework;

Agency	Title of Rule (RIN)	Date Published	Cost-Benefit Analysis Information Provided in GAO Report
Department of Education			increased clarity about incentive compensation for employees at institutions of higher education; reporting of information on program completers for programs leading to gainful employment, including costs, debt levels, graduation rates, and placement rates; the establishment of minimum standards for credit hours; greater transparency for borrowers participating in the programs offered under written agreements between institutions; greater detail about misrepresentation in marketing and recruitment materials; a more structured and consistent approach to the development and implementation of satisfactory academic progress policies; updated and simplified procedures for verifying Free Application for Federal Student Aid (FAFSA) applicant information; updated regulations related to the return of title IV of the Higher Education Act, as amended, (title IV, HEA) funds when a student withdraws; harmonization of Direct Loan and Teach Grant disbursement procedures with other title IV, HEA programs; and revised disbursement requirements to ensure Federal Pell Grant recipients can access funds in a timely manner.

Table A-1. (Continued)

Agency	Title of Rule (RIN)	Date Published	Cost-Benefit Analysis Information Provided in GAO Report
Department of Transportation, Federal Highway Administration	Real-Time System Management Information Program (2125-AF19)	11/8/2010	FHWA analyzed the costs and benefits of this final rule. FHWA determined that this final rule will not adversely affect, in a material way, any sector of the economy and estimates that the net present value of the estimated costs and benefits through 2021 represents at least a $315 million benefit to American travelers and taxpayers, corresponding to a benefit-cost ratio of 1.3. [DOT estimated the annualized cost of the rule at between $141.1 million and $145.9 million, and estimated the annualized benefits at between $162.3 million and $177.3 million.]
Department of Health and Human Services, Centers for Medicare & Medicaid Services	Medicare Program; Medicare Part B Monthly Actuarial Rates, Premium Rate, and Annual Deductible Beginning January 1, 2011 (0938-AP81)	11/9/2010	CMS estimates the standard Part B premium rate of $115.40 is $4.90 higher than the premium for 2010, so there will be about $700 million of additional costs in 2011 to the approximately 12 million Part B enrollees who pay the increase in the Part B premium.
Department of Health and Human Services, Centers for Medicare & Medicaid Services	Medicare Program; Inpatient Hospital Deductible and Hospital and Extended Care Services Coinsurance Amounts for CY2011 (0938-AP86)	11/9/2010	CMS estimates that the total increase in costs to beneficiaries is about $900 million due to the increase in the deductible and coinsurance amounts and the change in the number of deductibles and daily coinsurance amounts paid.

Agency	Title of Rule (RIN)	Date Published	Cost-Benefit Analysis Information Provided in GAO Report
Securities and Exchange Commission	Regulation SHO (3235-AK35)	11/9/2010	The Commission generally considers the costs and benefits of its rules. According to the Commission, the delay of the compliance date for the amendments to Rule 201 and Rule 200(g) of Regulation SHO will delay the benefits of the rules, but will also delay the ongoing costs of complying with the amendments. The Commission determined that the limited extension is necessary and appropriate because it will provide certain exchanges additional time to modify their current procedures for conducting single-priced transactions for covered securities that have triggered Rule 201's circuit breakers in a manner that is consistent with the goals and requirements of Rule 201, and industry participants additional time for programming and testing for compliance with the requirements of Rule 201 and Rule 200(g).
Securities and Exchange Commission	Risk Management Controls for Brokers or Dealers With Market Access (3235-AK53)	11/15/2010	The Securities and Exchange Commission (Commission) analyzed the costs and benefits of this final rule. The Commission expects that this final rule will benefit investors, broker-dealers, their counterparties, and the national market system as a whole by reducing the risks faced by broker-dealers and other market participants as a result of various market access arrangements by requiring financial and regulatory risk management controls to be implemented on a uniform, market-wide basis.

Table A-1. (Continued)

Agency	Title of Rule (RIN)	Date Published	Cost-Benefit Analysis Information Provided in GAO Report
Securities and Exchange Commission			A specific benefit identified by the Commission is a reduction of systemic risk associated with market access through the elimination of "unfiltered" or "naked" access. The Commission estimates that the total annual initial cost for all broker-dealers will be approximately $114.4 million and that the total annual ongoing cost for all 1,375 broker-dealers will be approximately $112.9 million.
Department of Defense, Office of the Secretary	Homeowners Assistance Program—Application Processing (0790-AI58)	11/16/2010	In its submission to the Comptroller General, DOD did not include a cost-benefit analysis of the final rule.
Department of Health and Human Services, Centers for Medicare & Medicaid Services	Medicare Program; Home Health Prospective Payment System Rate Update for Calendar Year 2011; Changes in Certification Requirements for Home Health Agencies and Hospices (0938-AP88)	11/17/2010	CMS prepared a cost-benefit analysis in conjunction with the final rule. CMS estimates that the net impact of the final rule will be approximately $960 million in CY2011 savings. CMS estimates the distributional effects of an updated wage index will account for a $20 million increase, the 1.1 percent home health market basket update will account for a $210 million increase, while the 3.79 percent casemix adjustment applicable to the national standardized 60-day episode rates will account for a $700 million decrease, and the 2.5 percent returned form the outlier provisions of the Affordable Care Act will result in a $490 million decrease.

Agency	Title of Rule (RIN)	Date Published	Cost-Benefit Analysis Information Provided in GAO Report
Department of Health and Human Services, Centers for Medicare & Medicaid Services	Medicare Program: Hospital Outpatient Prospective Payment System and CY2011 Payment Rates; Ambulatory Surgical Center Payment System and CY2011 Payment Rates; Payments to Hospitals for Graduate Medical Education Costs; Physician Self- Referral Rules and Related Changes to Provider Agreement Regulations; Payment for Certified Registered Nurse Anesthetist Services Furnished in Rural Hospitals and Critical Access Hospitals (0938-AP82; 0938- AP80)	11/24/2010	CMS performed a cost-benefit analysis of the final rule with comment period. CMS estimates that the total increase (from changes in the final rule with comment period as well as enrollment, utilization, and case-mix changes) in expenditures under the hospital outpatient prospective payment system (OPPS) for calendar year (CY) 2011 compared to CY2010 will be approximately $3.2 billion. CMS also estimates that the total increase (from changes in the final rule with comment period as well as enrollment, utilization, and case-mix changes) in expenditures under the ambulatory surgical center (ASC) payment system provisions for CY2011 compared to CY2010 will be approximately $230 million.
Department of Health and Human Services, Centers for Medicare & Medicaid Services	Medicare Program; Payment Policies Under the Physician Fee Schedule and Other Revisions to Part B for CY2011 (0938-AP79)	11/29/2010	CMS prepared a cost-benefit analysis of the final rule. CMS estimates that the final rule will result in a decrease in expenditures of $17.6 billion for physician fee schedule (PFS) conversion factor update. CMS estimates an increase in expenditures of $1.97 billion for Affordable Care Act provisions.
Department of Health and Human Services	Health Insurance Issuers Implementing Medical Loss Ratio (MLR) Requirements Under the Patient Protection and Affordable Care Act (0950-AA06)	12/1/2010	In developing this interim final regulation, HHS considered its potential effects including both costs and benefits. Because of data limitations, HHS did not attempt to quantify the benefits of this regulation. Nonetheless, HHS was able to identify several potential benefits.

Table A-1. (Continued)

Agency	Title of Rule (RIN)	Date Published	Cost-Benefit Analysis Information Provided in GAO Report
Department of Health and Human Services			HHS believes one potential benefit to this regulation is greater market transparency and improved ability of consumers to make informed insurance choices. In addition, HHS states that issuers that would not otherwise meet the MLR minimum defined by this regulation may increase spending on quality-promoting activities. According to HHS, these programs, which include case management, care coordination, chronic disease management and medication compliance, have the potential to create a societal benefit by improving outcomes and population health. HHS notes that issuers that would not otherwise meet the MLR minimum may also expand covered benefits or reduce cost sharing. HHS believes that to the extent that these changes result in increased consumption of effective health services, the regulation could result in improved health outcomes, thereby creating a societal benefit. HHS has identified the primary sources of costs associated with this regulation as the costs associated with reporting, recordkeeping, rebate notifications and payments, and other costs.

Agency	Title of Rule (RIN)	Date Published	Cost-Benefit Analysis Information Provided in GAO Report
Department of Health and Human Services			HHS estimates that issuers will incur approximately $33 million to $67 million in one-time administrative costs, and $11 million to $29 million in annual ongoing administrative costs related to complying with the requirements of this interim final regulation from 2011 through 2013. HHS notes that there are two other potential types of costs associated with this regulation: costs of potential increases in medical care use, the cost of additional quality-improving activities, and costs to consumers if some issuers decide to limit offered products as a result of this interim final regulation.
Department of Veterans Affairs	Payment for Inpatient and Outpatient Health Care Professional Services at Non- Departmental Facilities and Other Medical Charges Associated With Non-VA Outpatient Care (2900-AN37)	12/17/2010	VA performed a cost-benefit analysis in conjunction with the final rule. VA analyzed the expected savings from using the Medicare outpatient payment methodologies rather than the current VA method in four different categories. VA determined the cost reduction for clinical lab claims, as a percentage of payments made under current VA methodology, would be 74.6 percent. The cost reduction for outpatient dialysis facility claims would be 38.8 percent. The cost reduction for non-VA ambulatory surgery center claims would be 11.2 percent. And finally, the cost reduction for non-VA hospital outpatient department and emergency room facility claims would be 33.2 percent.

Table A-1. (Continued)

Agency	Title of Rule (RIN)	Date Published	Cost-Benefit Analysis Information Provided in GAO Report
Department of Veterans Affairs			VA estimates that the annual savings resulting from adoption of Medicare pricing standards for payment of outpatient services to be $274.6 million in fiscal year 2011, and approximately $1.8 billion total over the next five fiscal years.
Department of the Treasury	Management of Federal Agency Disbursements (1510-AB26)	12/22/2010	GAO's website does not contain a major rule report for this rule. However, in the rule itself, Treasury estimated the benefits of the rule at $117 million reduced costs to the federal government.
Consumer Product Safety Commission	Safety Standards for Full-Size Baby Cribs and Non-Full Size Baby Cribs	12/28/2010	The final rule does not include a cost-benefit analysis. However, the Commission estimated a total onetime cost to child care centers of $97 million nationwide for replacing all of their full-size cribs, and a one-time cost of $290 million nationwide for replacing all of their non-full-size cribs. The Commission determined that the impact on child care centers, family child care homes, and places of public accommodation could be significant and provides a 6-month effective date with an additional 18-month compliance period for these entities to meet the standard.

Source: CRS, using the GAO Federal Rules Database, located at http://www.gao.gov/fedrules/.

Note: For the analysis in the text of this report, when the GAO report did not provide sufficient information to discern the costs and benefits of the rule, CRS consulted the rules themselves.

End Notes

[1] 5 U.S.C. § 801(a)(1)(A). For more information on the CRA, see CRS Report RL31160, *Disapproval of Regulations by Congress: Procedure Under the Congressional Review Act*, by Richard S. Beth; and CRS Report RL30116, *Congressional Review of Agency Rulemaking: An Update and Assessment of The Congressional Review Act after a Decade*, by Morton Rosenberg.

[2] 5 U.S.C. §801(a)(3).

[3] 5 U.S.C. § 801(a)(2)(A). To access these reports, see http://www.gao.gov/decisions/majrule/majrule.php. In the reports, GAO generally summarizes the agencies' economic analyses, and does not prepare its own analysis.

[4] 5 U.S.C. § 804(2).

[5] In 2001, Congress disapproved a rule on ergonomics in the workplace. See U.S. Department of Labor, Occupational Safety and Health Administration, "Ergonomics Program," 65 *Federal Register* 68261, November 14, 2000. Although the CRA has been used to disapprove only one rule, it may have other, less direct or discernable effects (e.g., keeping Congress informed about agency rulemaking and preventing the publication of rules that may be disapproved).

[6] Although Congress has used the CRA to disapprove only one rule, Congress regularly uses appropriations restrictions to prevent certain proposed rules from becoming final, or to prevent the implementation of particular final rules. See CRS Report RL 34354, *Congressional Influence on Rulemaking and Regulation Through Appropriations Restrictions*, by Curtis W. Copeland.

[7] As of February 18, 2011, the REINS Act had been referred to the House Judiciary Committee's Subcommittee on Courts, Commercial and Administrative Law and the Senate Committee on Homeland Security and Governmental Affairs.

[8] H.R. 10, Section 2. Section 2 of S. 299 contains the same language, although separated into different numbered paragraphs.

[9] Anonymous, "The Congressional Accountability Act," *Wall Street Journal*, January 14, 2011, p. A14.

[10] Wayne Crews, "Tyranny of the Unelected; Congress Needs to Get a Handle on Costly Rules," *Washington Times*, October 12, 2010, p. B.1. Others have made similar comments. For example, an editorial in the *Las Vegas Review-Journal* ("Too Many Rules," January 24, 2011, p. B9) stated that the REINS Act requires an up-or-down vote on "regulations likely to cost $100 million or more...."

[11] Phil Kerpin, "Regulatory State Needs More Than a Trim; First a Red-Tape Timeout Before Adding New Restraints," *Washington Times*, January 24, 2011, p. B3.

[12] See http://judiciary p. 6.

[13] Sidney Shapiro, "The REINS Act: The Latest Conservatives Plan to Gum Up the Regulatory Works," January 14, 2011, available at http://www.progressivereform.org/CPRBlog.cfm?idBlog=84F5CF0B-E804-F8D1-7197786456C5DC4F.

[14] See http://judiciary p. 2. See also, Cheryl Bolen, "Congressional Approval of Major Rules Brings Partisan Jabs at Oversight Hearing," *BNA Daily Report for Executives*, January 25, 2010, p. A-21.

[15] E-mails of January 26, 2011, and February 1, 2011, to the deputy administrator of OIRA, and an official in the OMB Office of the General Counsel.

[16] Telephone conversation with Michael Fitzpatrick, associate administrator of OIRA, February 18, 2011.

[17] According to the Office of the Federal Register, the preamble to a final rule contains information about the basis and purpose of the rule, but does not include the regulatory text. For more information, see the *Federal Register Document Drafting Handbook, at* http://www.archives.gov/federal-register/write/handbook/chapter-2.pdf, p. 2-6.

[18] "The Congressional Accountability Act," *Wall Street Journal*, January 14, 2011, p. A14.

[19] Susan E. Dudley, "President Obama's Executive Order: Improving Regulation and Regulatory Review," January 18 2011, available at http://www.regulatorystudies.gwu.edu/images. These numbers have also been cited by others in congressional testimony. See testimony of Thomas M. Sullivan before the Subcommittee on the Courts, Commercial and Administrative Law, House Committee on the Judiciary, February 10, 2011, p. 6, available at http://judiciary

[20] For example, in testimony before the House Committee on Oversight and Government Reform on February 10, 2011, James Gattuso, Senior Research Fellow in Regulatory Policy for the Heritage Foundation, stated that "Last year...the number and cost of new regulations imposed by federal agencies reached unprecedented levels." He also said that federal agencies had issued 43 major rules during FY2010 that were "increasing regulatory burdens." See http://oversight to view a copy of this testimony. The statements were referenced to a study by Mr. Gattuso and two co-authors entitled "Red Tape Rising: Obama's Torrent of New Regulations," available at http://www.heritage.org/research/reports/2010/10/red-taperising-obamas-torrent-of-new-regulation. GAO's database indicates that federal agencies issued 104 major rules during FY2010.

[21] The definition of a "major rule" in the CRA was taken from Executive Order 12291, which was abolished when Executive Order 12866 was issued in September 1993. Data from the Regulatory Information Service Center (at http://www.reginfo.gov) indicates that OIRA reviewed an average of 67 "economically significant" or "major" regulatory actions per year from 1982 through 1996, but that average includes both proposed and final rules.

[22] Of the 16 major rules that were published in the *Federal Register* during January 2009, the GAO database indicates that 11 of them were published on or before January 21, 2009. Although President Obama was sworn into office on January 20, 2009, the rules that were published on January 21 (including one major rule) had already been submitted to the Office of the Federal Register.

[23] See, for example, OMB's *2010 Report to Congress on the Benefits and Costs of Federal Regulations and Unfunded Mandates on State, Local, and Tribal Entities*, available at http://www.whitehouse.gov/sites/default/files/omb/legislative/reports/2010_Benefit_Cost_Report.pdf. On p. 10 of that report, OMB stated that certain rules were considered major rules "primarily due to their impact on the economy (i.e., estimated benefits or costs were in excess of $100 million in at least one year)." The report also indicated that other rules were considered major because of federal and non-federal transfers, consumer surpluses (also referred to as "consumer welfare increase"), and non-monetized impacts. Within the category of "transfer rules" were rules setting fees from program beneficiaries.

[24] Thirty-four of the rules appeared to be "major" only because of transfers, and three rules involved transfers and one other category of explanation. OMB's *2010 Report to Congress on the Benefits and Costs of Federal Regulations and Unfunded Mandates on State, Local, and Tribal Entities* notes (on p. 21) that transfer rules "may impose real costs on society to the extent that they cause people to change behavior, either by directly prohibiting or

mandating certain activities, or, more often, by altering prices and costs. The costs resulting from these behavior changes are referred to as 'deadweight loss' associated with the transfer."

[25] U.S. Department of Energy, "Weatherization Assistance Program for Low-Income Persons," 75 *Federal Register* 3847, January 25, 2010. DOE stated (p. 3854) that the $5 billion in grants for the weatherization program "at a level greater than $100 million makes this rulemaking economically significant under [Executive Order 12866]." As noted later in this report, the definition a "major rule" in the CRA is slightly broader than the definition of "economically significant" in the executive order. DOE also indicated (on p. 3856) that the rule was "major" under the CRA.

[26] U.S. Department of Agriculture, Food and Nutrition Service, "Food Stamp Program: Eligibility and Certification Provisions of the Farm Security and Rural Investment Act of 2002; Final Rule," 75 *Federal Register* 4911, January 29, 2010.

[27] U.S. Department of Education, Office of Innovation and Improvement, "Investing in Innovation Fund; Final Rule and Notice," 75 *Federal Register* 12003, March 12, 2010.

[28] U.S. Department of Defense, Office of the Secretary, "Retroactive Stop Loss Special Pay Compensation," 75 *Federal Register* 19878, April 16, 2010. For more information on the stop loss special pay program, see http://www.defense.gov/home/features/2010/0710_stoploss/.

[29] U.S. Department of Health and Human Services, "Medicare Program; Hospice Wage Index for Fiscal Year 2011; Notice," 75 *Federal Register* 42943, July 22, 2010.

[30] U.S. Department of Health and Human Services, Office of Consumer Information and Insurance Oversight, "Pre-Existing Condition Insurance Plan Program," 75 Federal Register 45013, July 30, 2010.

[31] U.S. Department of Veterans Affairs, "Diseases Associated With Exposure to Certain Herbicide Agents (Hairy Cell Leukemia and Other Chronic B-Cell Leukemias, Parkinson's Disease and Ischemic Heart Disease)," 75 *Federal Register* 53202, August 31, 2010.

[32] U.S. Department of Agriculture, Farm Service Agency, "Crop Assistance Program," 75 *Federal Register* 65423, October 25, 2010.

[33] U.S. Department of Homeland Security, Federal Emergency Management Agency, "Special Community Disaster Loans Program," 75 *Federal Register* 2800, January 19, 2010. FEMA stated (p. 2815) that although "the impact of the rule could be spread over multiple years as applications are received, processed, and loans cancelled, the total economic effects of a specific loan cancellation would occur once, rather than annually."

[34] Seven of these rules appeared to be "major" only because of decreased transfers, and two other rules involved decreased transfers and one other category of explanation.

[35] U.S. Department of Health and Human Services, Centers for Medicare and Medicaid Services, "Medicare Program; End-Stage Renal Disease Prospective Payment System; Final Rule and Proposed Rule," 75 *Federal Register* 49029, August 25, 2010.

[36] U.S. Department of Health and Human Services, Centers for Medicare and Medicaid Services, "Medicare Program; Hospital Inpatient Prospective Payment Systems for Acute Care Hospitals and the Long-Term Care Hospital Prospective Payment System Changes and FY2011 Rates; Provider Agreements and Supplier Approvals; and Hospital Conditions of Participation for Rehabilitation and Respiratory Care Services; Medicaid Program: Accreditation for Providers of Inpatient Psychiatric Services," 75 *Federal Register* 50041, August 16, 2010.

[37] U.S. Department of Defense, Office of the Secretary, "Civilian Health and Medical Program of the Uniformed Services (CHAMPUS)/TRICARE: Inclusion of TRICARE Retail Pharmacy

Program in Federal Procurement of Pharmaceuticals," 75 *Federal Register* 63383, October 15, 2010.

[38] Four of these rules appeared to be "major" only because of non-federal transfers, and one other rule also involved another category of explanation.

[39] U.S. Department of the Treasury, Internal Revenue Service; Department of Labor, Employee Benefits Security Administration; Department of Health and Human Services, Centers for Medicare and Medicaid Services, "Interim Final Rules Under the Paul Wellstone and Pete Domenici Mental Health Parity and Addiction Equity Act of 2008," 75 *Federal Register* 5409, February 2, 2010. Discounted benefits or costs are sometimes referred to as "discounted present values," or simply "present values," and are used when the costs and the benefits of rules are expected to occur at different times. OMB Circular A-4 recommends that agencies use both a 7% and a 3% discount rate. The annual undiscounted transfer estimates ranged from $2.36 billion to $2.81 billion per year.

[40] U.S. Department of the Treasury, Internal Revenue Service; Department of Labor, Employee Benefits Security Administration; Department of Health and Human Services, Centers for Medicare and Medicaid Services, "Group Health Plans and Health Insurance Issuers Relating to Dependent Coverage of Children to Age 26 Under the Patient Protection and Affordable Care Act," 75 *Federal Register* 27121, May 13, 2010.

[41] U.S. Department of Agriculture, Commodity Credit Corporation, "Conservation Reserve Program," 75 *Federal Register* 44067, July 28, 2010. According to the GAO major rule report, certain provisions in the rule would "largely substitute one [conservation reserve program] participant for another, or one practice for another, leading in a shift in costs and benefits to different participants and practices, but little net cost or benefit for the [commodity reserve program] as a whole."

[42] In this case, the consumer surplus is an estimate of the amount individuals are willing to pay to hunt waterfowl and other types of migratory birds.

[43] U.S. Department of the Interior, Fish and Wildlife Department, "Migratory Bird Hunting; Final Frameworks for Late-Season Migratory Bird Hunting Regulations," 75 *Federal Register* 58249, September 23, 2010.

[44] The REINS Act states that "any rule that establishes, modifies, opens, closes, or conducts a regulatory program for a commercial, recreational, or subsistence activity related to hunting, fishing, or camping... shall take effect at such time as the Federal agency promulgating the rule determines." Therefore, it appears that these migratory bird hunting rules would not be subject to congressional approval procedures before being allowed to take effect.

[45] U.S. Nuclear Regulatory Commission, "Revision of Fee Schedules; Fee Recovery for FY 2010," 75 *Federal Register* 34219, June 16, 2010

[46] U.S. Department of State, "Schedule of Fees for Consular Services, Department of State and Overseas Embassies and Consulates," 75 *Federal Register* 36522, June 28, 2010.

[47] U.S. Department of Homeland Security, U.S. Citizenship and Immigration Services, "U.S. Citizenship and Immigration Services Fee Schedule," 75 *Federal Register* 58961, September 24, 2010.

[48] Executive Order 12866, "Regulatory Planning and Review," 58 *Federal Register* 51735, October 4, 1993.

[49] Section 3(f)(1) of the executive order defines an economically significant rule as one that may "have an annual effect on the economy of $100 million or more or adversely affect in a material way the economy, a sector of the economy, productivity, competition, jobs, the environment, public health or safety, or State, local, or tribal governments or communities." In its guidance on the CRA, OMB said that the main difference between "economically

significant" and "major" rules is that some rules may be captured by the CRA definition that are not considered "economically significant" under EO12866, "notably those rules that would have a significant adverse effect on the ability of United States-based enterprises to compete with foreign-based enterprises in domestic and export markets." See http://www.whitehouse.gov/sites/default/files/omb/assets

[50] Thirty-seven of the rules appeared to be "major" only because of such costs and/or benefits, and two other rules also involved one other category of explanation.

[51] U.S. Environmental Protection Agency, "Primary National Ambient Air Quality Standards for Nitrogen Dioxide," 75 *Federal Register* 6473, February 9, 2010. Although EPA prepared a cost-benefit analysis for the rule, EPA said that the Clean Air Act and judicial decisions "make clear that the economic and technical feasibility of attaining ambient standards are not to be considered in setting or revising [national ambient air quality standards]."

[52] U.S. Environmental Protection Agency, "National Emission Standards for Hazardous Air Pollutants for Reciprocating Internal Combustion Engines," 75 *Federal Register* 9647, March 3, 2010.

[53] U.S. Department of Transportation, Federal Aviation Administration, "Automatic Dependent Surveillance— Broadcast (ADS-B) Out Performance Requirements To Support Air Traffic Control (ATC) Service," 75 *Federal Register* 30159, May 28, 2010.

[54] U.S. Department of Justice, Civil Rights Division, "Nondiscrimination on the Basis of Disability in State and Local Government Services," 75 *Federal Register* 56163, September 15, 2010.

[55] U.S. Department of Energy, Office of Energy Efficiency and Renewable Energy, "Energy Conservation Program: Energy Conservation Standards for Small Electric Motors," 75 *Federal Register* 10873, March 9, 2010.

[56] U.S. Department of Health and Human Services, Food and Drug Administration, "Regulations Restricting the Sale and Distribution of Cigarettes and Smokeless Tobacco To Protect Children and Adolescents," 61 *Federal Register* 44569, March 19, 2010.

[57] Department of Transportation, Federal Motor Carrier Safety Administration, "Electronic On-Board Recorders for Hours-of-Service Compliance," 75 *Federal Register* 17207, April 5, 2010.

[58] Department of Energy, "Energy Conservation Program: Energy Conservation Standards for Residential Water Heaters, Direct Heating Equipment, and Pool Heaters," 75 *Federal Register* 20112, April 16, 2010.

[59] U.S. Department of Labor, Occupational Safety and Health Administration, "Cranes and Derricks in Construction," 75 *Federal Register* 47905, August 9, 2010.

[60] U.S. Department of Transportation, Federal Railroad Administration, "Positive Train Control Systems," 75 *Federal Register* 2598, January 15, 2010. "Positive train control systems" refers to technology that can prevent accidents such as train-to-train collisions and train movements through a switch left in the wrong position.

[61] U.S. Department of Transportation, Federal Railroad Administration, "Positive Train Control Systems," 75 *Federal Register* 2598, January 15, 2010, p. 2685.

[62] U.S. Securities and Exchange Commission, "Custody of Funds or Securities of Clients by Investment Advisers," 75 *Federal Register*, 1455, January 11, 2010.

[63] U.S. Department of Health and Human Services, Food and Drug Administration, "Use of Ozone-Depleting Substances; Removal of Essential-Use Designation (Flunisolide, etc.)," 75 *Federal Register* 19213, April 14, 2010.

[64] The agency indicated that the rule could add more than 5 million hours of annual paperwork burden. Using OMB's estimate of the cost of completing this paperwork of $30 per hour, compliance costs would exceed $100 million.

[65] U.S. Department of Education, Office of Postsecondary Education, "Program Integrity Issues," 75 *Federal Register* 66831, October 29, 2010.

[66] Sixteen of the rules only had this effect, and one rule also appeared to be major for another reason.

[67] Department of Agriculture, Agricultural Marketing Service, "National Organic Program; Access to Pasture (Livestock)," 75 *Federal Register* 7154, February 17, 2010.

[68] Securities and Exchange Commission, "Political Contributions by Certain Investment Advisers," 75 *Federal Register* 41018, July 14, 2010.

[69] Department of Labor, Employee Benefits Security Administration, "Reasonable Contract or Arrangement Under Section 408(b)(2)- Fee Disclosure," 75 *Federal Register* 41600, July 16, 2010.

[70] U.S. Department of the Treasury, Comptroller of the Currency and Office of Thrift Supervision; Federal Reserve System; Federal Deposit Insurance Corporation; Farm Credit Administration; and National Credit Union Administration, "Registration of Mortgage Loan Originators," 75 *Federal Register* 44655, July 28, 2010.

[71] Section 624 of the Treasury and General Government Appropriations Act, 2001 (P.L. 106-54).

[72] As noted earlier in this report, the definition of an "economically significant" rule under EO12866 is not as broad as the definition of a "major rule" under the CRA. The definition of a covered rule under the Unfunded Mandates Reform Act is much more narrow, excluding (among other things) rules issued without a prior notice of proposed rulemaking, rules that do not require $100 million in "expenditures" (instead of "costs"), and rules issued by independent regulatory agencies. See U.S. Government Accountability Office, *Unfunded Mandates: Analysis of Reform Act Coverage*, GAO-04-637, May 12, 2004.

[73] To view this report, see http://www.whitehouse.gov/sites/default/files/omb/legislative/reports/2010_Benefit_Cost_Report.pdf.

[74] One of these rules was an NRC fee recovery schedule for FY2009, so the "costs" were likely the fees recovered from the licensees and others for the operation of the program.

[75] The one exception was an SEC rule in which OMB said the agency provided benefit and cost estimates, but OMB did not include them in its report.

[76] The George W. Bush Administration was also described as increasing the number of rules and major rules. See Veronique de Rugy, "Bush's Regulatory Kiss-Off," *Reason.com*, January 2009, available at http://reason.com/archives/ 2008/12/10/bushs-regulatory-kiss-off, which said that there had been a "significant increase in regulatory activity and cost since 2001."

[77] "The Congressional Accountability Act," *Wall Street Journal*, January 14, 2011, p. A14. Others have also indicated that the number of rules issued during the Obama Administration had risen sharply. See also Jennifer Rubin, "Change Comes in the Form of Congressional Oversight," *Washington Post*, January 27, 2011, available at http://voices.washingtonpost.com/right-turn/2011/01/change_congressional_oversight

[78] Wayne Crews, "Tyranny of the Unelected; Congress Needs to Get a Handle on Costly Rules," *Washington Times*, October 12, 2010, p. B.1, in which the author states that Congress need not approve all rules, "just the 'major' one costing more than $100 million annually, of which there are less than 200 each year." See also an editorial in the *Las Vegas Review-Journal* ("Too Many Rules," January 24, 2011, p. B9), which stated that the REINS Act requires an up-or-down vote on "regulations likely to cost $100 million or more...." Also, in testimony before the House Judiciary Committee's Subcommittee on the Courts and

Commercial and Administrative Law on January 24, 2011, former Representative David McIntosh said that major rules are "those projected to impose cost on the American economy of more than $100 million each." See
http://judiciary

[79] U.S. Department of Transportation, Federal Railroad Administration, "Positive Train Control Systems," 75 *Federal Register* 2598, January 15, 2010, p. 2685.

In: Federal Government and the REINS Act ISBN: 978-1-62100-346-5
Editors: L. Matthews and J. Fanning

Chapter 2

TESTIMONY OF DAVID MCINTOSH BEFORE THE SUBCOMMITTEE ON COURTS, COMMERCIAL AND ADMINISTRATIVE LAW OF THE HOUSE JUDICIARY COMMITTEE, HEARING ON "THE REINS ACT - PROMOTING JOBS AND EXPANDING FREEDOM BY REDUCING NEEDLESS REGULATIONS"*

The 112th Congress, January 24, 2011

Restoring Democracy in the Regulatory Process

Chairman Coble and Ranking Member Cohen and Members of the Subcommittee, thank you for the opportunity to appear before you today. I am appearing in my own capacity and not representing any other person.[1] Your hearing raises some of the most important issues facing the nation today: Does our current regulatory system undermine economic recovery and hold the private sector back from creating new jobs? And, how can we reform the

---

* **This is an edited, reformatted and augmented version of testimony given by David McIntosh before the Subcommittee on Courts, Commercial and Administrative Law of the House Judiciary Committee, Hearing on "The REINS Act - Promoting Jobs and Expanding Freedom by Reducing Needless Regulations" on January 24, 2011.**

regulatory process to provide more accountability and encourage better regulations that reduce their costs, thereby unleashing economic growth and the creation of more jobs?

I want to commend the Committee for taking up this topic and also applaud Representative Geoff Davis and his co-sponsors for introducing the Regulations from the Executive In Need of Scrutiny (REINS) Act (H.R. 10). As I will discuss today in my testimony, the REINS Act as it has come to be known provides an excellent opportunity for Congress to restore accountability for regulatory decisions. In addition, it corrects significant flaws in the current regulatory system — including Constitutional issues that may arise from the improper delegation of legislative authority under the current structure. The REINS Act is also a logical next step to build upon the Congressional Review Act.

In this testimony I hope to present to the Committee several points that I hope will be useful as it pursues its oversight of the regulatory process and considers this legislation: I. The current burden of Federal regulations is unprecedented and clearly has impeded efforts to stimulate economic growth and job creation. 2. The Congressional Review Act serves several useful purposes and should be employed by the Congress in considering new regulations promulgated by the Administration. At the same time, there is a pressing need for Congress to create a structure that ensures greater oversight of the regulatory process and accurately reflects the legislative will of the people. 3. The REINS Act provides the proper mechanism for ensuring that legislative power under Article I remains in Congress, which will have full accountability as a democratically elected body to the citizens of the United States for the broad range of policies implemented by major regulations.

Unprecedented Economic Burden of Federal Regulations

In the first two years of the Obama Administration, we have seen an unprecedented level of regulatory activity. In 2009 and 2010, the number of major rulemakings — those projected to impose cost on the American economy of more than $100 million each — that were announced by various agencies averaged 66 per year. That is a 38% increase from the average number of major rulemakings in the Bush and Clinton Administrations.[2]

This high pace of regulatory activity imposes a huge cost onto the American economy. Last year Federal regulations were estimated by the Obama Administration to cost U.S. consumers, businesses, and workers $1.75 trillion annually.[3] For comparison, $1.75 trillion is nearly twice the amount of all individual income taxes collected last year.[4] It is estimated that the overall cost of Federal regulation is over $15,000 per household in the United States.[5] Not only is this a significant drain on the wallets and pocket books of working American families, as I will discuss below, it is a significant restraint on economic growth needed to restore full employment.

Those agencies that reported costs — by all means not all the significant regulations — reported a total of $28 billion in new additional costs last year.[6] This is the highest level since such statistics have been compiled. According to the Heritage Foundation analysis, fifteen of these rulemaking procedures involved *financial* regulations. Another five stem from the healthcare bill adopted in early 2010. Ten others came from the Environmental Protection Agency (EPA). Among the most costly are[7]:

- Fuel economy and emission standards[8] for passenger cars, light-duty trucks, and medium-duty passenger vehicles imposed jointly by the EPA and NHTSA.[9] Annual cost: $10.8 billion (for model years 2012 to 2016). For automakers to recover these increased outlays, NHTSA estimates the standards will lead to increases in average new vehicle prices ranging from $457 per vehicle in FY 2012 to $985 per vehicle in FY 2016.
- Mandated quotas for renewable fuels.[10] Annual cost: $7.8 billion (for 15 years). Utilizing farmland to grow corn and other crops used in renewable fuels will displace food crops, leading food costs to increase by $10 per person per year — or $40 for a family of four, according to the EPA.
- Efficiency standards *for residential* water heaters, heating equipment, and pool heaters.[11] Annual cost: $1.3 billion. The appliance upgrades necessary to comply with the new standards will raise the price of a typical gas storage water heater by $120.

The trend of increasing regulatory burden will continue to worsen in 2011. The Dodd-Frank bill requires eleven different Federal agencies to promulgate 243 new formal rules.[12] The Congressional Research Service reports that the newly-enacted healthcare legislation has at least 43 provisions that create rule-making authority. These include mandatory rulemaking, disclosure rulemaking, procedure rulemaking, negotiating rulemaking, and other regulatory provisions.[13]

On December 21, 2010, the Federal Communications Commission issued its new neutrality regulation championed by Chairman Genachowski. As Commissioner Robert McDowell noted in his dissent, this regulation will cause irreparable harm to one of the most significant drivers of our modern economy. In the name of maintaining competition the rule will do the exact opposite and lead to: "Less investment. Less innovation.

Increased business costs. Increased prices for consumers. Disadvantages to smaller ISPs. Jobs lost." [14]

Economists have long understood the harm to economic growth and productivity that results from costly and unnecessary regulations.[15]

In particular, as Congress considers various new proposals to encourage job creation, it must take a critical look at regulations that make it more expensive for small and large businesses to create new jobs.

Federal regulations have a significant impact on businesses' decisions to hire more employees. For large firms the regulatory cost is $7,755 per employee. For medium-sized firms it is $7,454 per employee. Small firms are particularly hard hit. It costs them on average $10,585 per employee.[16]

Current Congressional Oversight of Regulations

When I began my service in Congress in 1995, Congress had essentially three means of exerting oversight of policies developed by regulatory agency, The first was through the committees of legislative jurisdiction, which typically maintain continuous informal communication with regulatory agencies and have the authority to work on substantive legislation defining the scope of regulatory powers of agencies whose programs fall under the committees' jurisdiction. In other words, if Congress determined that a particular regulation exceeds Congressional intent, the committee of jurisdiction could and often would begin a legislative process to change the enabling legislation that *authorizes* the regulatory *agency* to promulgate legislations.

A second, more expeditious way Congress exerted its authority was to hold oversight hearings and question the regulatory agency officials and invited witnesses about the wisdom of a given regulation. This oversight often had a significant influence on the agency's approach to developing its regulations.

The third means of influencing regulations is the appropriations rider that prohibits or limits agencies from spending funds in the development or enforcement of a given regulation. This relatively blunt policy instrument is a longstanding extension of Congress's power of the purse, by which all funds that are used to operate the Federal *Government* must be appropriated by the people's elected representatives.

In 1995, Congress passed and President Clinton signed the Congressional Review Act ("CRA"), which provided another mechanism for Congressional action on major[17] regulations. The CRA provides that a Federal rule cannot "take effect" until the agency promulgating the rule submits a report to each House of Congress and to the Government Accountability Office ("GAO") that includes (1) a copy *of* the *rule,* (2) a *description of the rule,* including a determination whether it is a "major rule," and (3) the proposed effective date. Rules that are not major rules take effect as otherwise provided by law after submission of the agency's report to Congress.

Major rules cannot take effect until 60 days after Congress receives the report from the agency or the rule is published in the Federal Register, whichever is later. The CRA provides expedited procedures for Congress to disapprove of an agency *rule* through the passage of a *joint resolution.* Some of the most significant provisions of the CRA create discharge procedures to bring the resolution of disapproval expeditiously to the House and Senate floors respectively. In the Senate, all points of order against the joint resolution, as well as against consideration of the resolution, are waived. The motion to proceed to the resolution is not subject to amendment or to a motion to postpone or proceed to the consideration of other business. A motion to reconsider the vote by which the motion is agreed to or disagreed to is not in order. If a motion to proceed to the consideration of the joint resolution is agreed to, the joint resolution remains the unfinished business of the Senate until final disposition of the resolution. Senate debate on the joint resolution, and on any debatable motions and appeals connected to the resolution, is limited to 10 hours.

Congress should make full use of the Congressional Review Act as it considers improvements in the regulatory process such as the REINS Act. The procedures will allow Members to ensure that there is healthy Congressional debate of regulations and the policies that are advanced by them.

Unfortunately, as time has gone on, some problems have been revealed in the implementation of the Congressional Review Act that the REINS Act would do a great deal to fix.

First, the default position of the Congressional Review Act is pro-regulatory. A regulation is presumptively authorized, and it will only be prevented from taking effect if Congress enacts a specific joint resolution to disapprove it. As everyone here knows, the inertia of the legislative process means that there is a big difference between requiring Congress to act and allowing Congress to stay silent. If Congress fails to address the regulation or is preoccupied with other matters, the rule — even a major rule — will still take effect, regardless of whether it could have survived on an up-or-down vote. Moreover, because both Houses must vote on a joint resolution of disapproval, if one House supports a rule and the other opposes it, a joint resolution of disapproval would fail, even if a joint resolution of *approval* could not be passed either. Under current law, in a case of disagreement between the Houses, the tie goes to the bureaucrats. The REINS Act would reverse that default by requiring an agency to get Congress's active permission to issue a major rule.

Second, the Congressional Review Act gives the President both too much and too little authority over regulation. If a major rule is proposed by an agency under the President's direct control, he presumably already favors the rule and could be expected to veto any joint resolution of disapproval. Stopping the rule would then require a *two-thirds* vote of both Houses. It's no surprise that the one time Congress has passed a resolution of disapproval, the 60-day review period spanned administrations, such that a major rule proposed under President Clinton was disapproved in a joint resolution signed by President George W. Bush. At the same time, however, *if* a major rule is proposed by one of the so-called independent agencies (as discussed below), the President may object strongly to the regulation, but he will have no opportunity to intervene unless Congress first pfesents him with a joint resolution of disapproval for his signature.

Third, and most importantly, the courts have deprived the CRA of any meaningful enforcement provisions. The CRA requires that each new rule be submitted to Congress "[b]efore [the] rule can take effect."[18] But government agencies have repeatedly failed to submit their rules as the Act requires, and have enforced those regulations against Americans anyway. According to the Congressional Research Service, from 1998 to 2008, Federal agencies failed to submit more than 1,000 substantive rules as required by the Act.[19]

The purpose of the Congressional Review Act was to give elected officials a say in whether Americans would be bound by new regulations. But when agencies ignore the CRA's procedures, there are no consequences. Congress is often too busy to notice the oversight, and when regulated parties challenge the regulations, the courts have refused to enforce the CRA's requirements. Instead, the courts have interpreted the judicial review provision of 5 U.S.C. § 805 to "specifically preclude[] judicial review *of an agency's* compliance with its terms."[20] Despite the law's clear requirements, Americans are forced to comply with regulations that have never been reviewed by Congress.

The REINS Act would give the existing approval process some teeth. Section 805(b) of the bill[21] adds a provision that "a court may determine whether a Federal agency has completed the necessary requirements under this chapter for a rule to take effect." As a result, if an agency tries to enforce a major rule without Congressional authorization, or shirks its duty to submit a non-major rule to Congress, the rule can be challenged in court and held invalid. This enforcement provision is a vital part of giving effect to existing law as well as bringing the regulatory apparatus under democratic control.

CONSTITUTIONALITY OF THE REINS ACT

The REINS Act would be a *fully constitutional exercise of* Congress's power to enact laws necessary and proper to the exercise of powers vested in the Federal Government. In addition, the bill would also help protect and enforce other provisions of the Constitution that have been eroded by the increasing power of administrative agencies.

A. The REINS Act Is Consistent with the Constitution

From a constitutional perspective, the REINS Act does three things. The bill (1) limits the statutory authority of administrative agencies to implement major rules; (2) provides a mechanism for Congress to authorize major rules on a rule-by-rule basis through joint resolutions of approval; and (3) creates a fast-track process enabling each House of Congress to vote on those confirmatory resolutions with a minimum of procedural delay. Each of these steps is itself consistent with the Constitution, and so is the process as a whole. Indeed, nearly twenty years ago Justice Stephen Breyer (then a judge on the U.S. Court of Appeals for the First Circuit) explained that a proposal like the

REINS Act would be consistent with the Constitution, in a way that other attempts at restraining agency discretion were not.[22]

1. Congress Has Power to Restrict Agency Authority to Implement Major Rules

The first aspect of the REINS Act is a limitation on the authority of administrative agencies to implement major rules. After the bill's passage, an agency with general power to regulate on a particular subject could not, of its own authority, implement any rule with a major effect on the U.S. economy. Instead, it would have to wait for Congress to grant permission on a rule-by-rule basis.

That limitation on agency power is undoubtedly constitutional. The Constitution grants Congress power "[t]o make all Laws which shall be necessary and proper for carrying into Execution" its enumerated legislative powers, as well as "all other Powers vested by this Constitution in the Government of the United States, or in any Department or Officer thereof."[23] Through the exercise of this power, Congress has created "a vast and varied federal bureaucracy."[24]

But because this discretion is vested in Congress, an agency "literally has no power to act * * * unless and until Congress confers power upon it."[25] An administrative agency "is entirely a creature of Congress" and can do only "what Congress has said it can do."[26] Thus, Congress has not only limited the substantive scope of agencies' authority to regulate on particular subjects, but has also required agencies to act only by the use of particular procedures (such as notice-and-comment rulemaking), or subject to particular decision-making constraints (such as by prohibiting agency action that is "arbitrary, capricious, [or] an abuse of discretion").[27] Similarly, Congress can require that an agency make decisions on the basis of particular types of reasons, such as by either forbidding or requiring the agency to take considerations *of economic* cost *into account* when formulating regulations.[28]

Here, Congress is imposing a different kind of limitation, one that addresses the *scale* of agency action — forbidding agencies, absent specific permission, to issue rules that have a major effect on the U.S. economy. That restriction is no different, constitutionally, from others that Congress has already enacted. In fact, the constraint is already present in current law in the form of the CRA, which prohibits agencies from implementing major rules without submitting them to Congress and postponing their implementation for a 60-day period of review. There is no constitutional distinction between requiring a 60-day waiting period and prohibiting the regulation from going into effect altogether. Rather, "Mt is axiomatic that an administrative agency's power to promulgate legislative regulations is limited to the authority delegated by Congress."[29]

Because the REINS Act addresses only one type of limitation on an agency's authority, it would preserve the protections of existing statutory restraints on agencies. When Congress authorizes a major rule through the REINS Act's procedures, it is authorizing the agency to implement a rule of a certain scale — not authorizing the rule in *all* of its respects, much less enacting the rule itself as a law. Congress has established many independent conditions that a rule must meet in order to have legal effect, and the REINS Act only addresses one of them. A rule that exceeds the scope of an agency's substantive authority, that was promulgated through improper *procedures,* or that violates an existing restraint on the agency's powers (such as a restriction on arbitrary or capricious action) is invalid.

Such a rule would not be made valid by the passage of a joint resolution of approval under the REINS Act. Under section 802(g) of the bill, the confirmatory resolution "does not serve as a grant * * * of statutory authority" and does not "extinguish" any "substantive or procedural" claim based on an "alleged defect in a rule." This provision avoids any risk that agencies will abuse the fast-track procedure to bypass the normal *legislative* process, proposing rules that go beyond their existing authority and that would otherwise require new laws to become effective.

That said, even if Congress's approval does not immunize a rule from challenge on these grounds, nothing prevents Congress from considering such grounds as a reason *not* to approve a rule. If a major rule appears to be arbitrary and capricious, or is contrary to law, or was imposed through improper procedures, that is a perfectly legitimate basis for Congress to decide not to authorize it. The REINS Act therefore serves as an additional check, preventing agencies from imposing unlawful regulations on the American people.

2. Congress Has Power to Enact Legislation Authorizing Individual Major Rules

The second aspect of the REINS Act is the passage of joint resolutions, on a rule-by-rule basis, to authorize the adoption of major rules. Each of these resolutions would be supported by the same enumerated power underlying the administrative rule itself. Moreover, the process of passage and individual review also satisfies the Constitution's requirements.

There is nothing unusual, constitutionally speaking, about the Executive's suggesting that Congress authorize the implementation of an individual rule. Under Article II, Section 3, the President is obliged "from time to time" to provide information to Congress and to "recommend to their Consideration such Measures as he shall judge necessary and expedient" Under the REINS Act, the President — through his subordinates in an administrative agency — would recommend that Congress grant authority to implement a particular major rule. Approving that individual regulation through a confirmatory resolution would be no more problematic than *disapproving* the same regulation through a resolution passed under the existing text of the CRA.

More importantly, the REINS Act provides for the enactment of that joint resolution in the constitutionally required way: passage by both Houses of Congress and presentment to the President. A joint resolution that confers authority on an agency is an exercise of legislative power. By empowering an agency to implement a rule that would otherwise be unauthorized, the resolution is "essentially legislative in purpose and effect."[30] Because the Constitution *vests* "[a]ll] legislative Powers herein granted" in Congress, "consist[ing] of [the] Senate and House of Representatives," it is necessary that both Houses vote to enact the confirmatory resolution.[31] The REINS Act procedure also complies with the *presentment requirements* of *Article* I, Section 7, namely that "[e]very Bill which shall have passed the House of Representatives and the Senate, shall, before it become a Law, be presented to the President of the United States" for his signature or veto — and that "[e]very Order, Resolution, or Vote to which the Concurrence of the Senate and House of Representatives may be necessary * * * be presented to the President" in the same manner as a bill.[32]

By requiring the proper enactment *of legislation in* the manner prescribed in the Constitution, the REINS Act stands in stark contrast to some previous attempts by Congress to restrain the discretion of administrative agencies. After the New Deal, Congress frequently attempted to impose a "legislative veto" on agency decision-making, whereby a single House of Congress (or sometimes both Houses together) could vote to bar an agency from taking action that the agency was otherwise authorized to take. These legislative vetoes were recognized as unconstitutional in the *Chadha* decision in 1983, which concerned the House of Representatives' veto of the Attorney General's decision to allow a deportable immigrant to remain in the United States.[33] As the Supreme Court pointed out, Congress's previous "choice to delegate authority to an agency" (here the Attorney General) had been given the force of law by enactment "in accordance with the procedures set out in Art. 1."[34] As a result, "Congress must abide by its delegation of authority until that delegation is legislatively altered or revoked."[35] Because the Constitution requires that "no law [may] take effect without the concurrence * * * of both Houses," and that "all legislation [must] be presented to the President before becoming law," a vote of a *single* House, or *of* both Houses without presentment to the President, was insufficient to override the previous grant of legal authority.[36] As the Court later put it in *Bowsher v. Synar,* "once Congress makes its choice in enacting legislation," it can "thereafter control the execution of its enactment only * * * by passing new legislation."[37]

The same reasons why the legislative veto was struck down in *Chadha* explain why the REINS Act procedures pass constitutional muster. Unlike the legislative veto, the REINS Act requires both bicameral agreement of the Houses and formal presentment to the President. A joint resolution under the REINS Act *is not* merely an expression *of* the *opinion of* a single House, but a valid exercise of the legislative power vested in Congress and exercised through the mechanism of Article I, Section 7. As such, the new legislation can override the previous limitation on agency authority by granting permission to implement a particular major rule. The REINS Act therefore satisfies the requirement that Congress "pass[] new legislation" in order to "control the execution" of old legislation.[38]

Indeed, in a lecture given shortly after the opinion issued in *Chadha,* then-Judge Stephen Breyer outlined a version of the REINS Act as a constitutional replacement for the legislative veto. As Breyer explained, by enacting limitations on an "agency's exercise of * * * authority," Congress could make new rules "ineffective unless Congress enacts a confirmatory law within" a set period of time.[39] Consistently with the Constitution, "Congress could" then "condition[] the legal *effect* of exercises of authority on subsequent enactment of a confirmatory statute."[40] (Breyer even noted the possibility of a special fast-track procedure to avoid delay.[41]) Because the REINS Act uses, rather than evades, the required procedures for enacting legislation, it would avoid the defects that imperiled the legislative veto.

Functionally, of course, there are certain similarities between the REINS Act and the unconstitutional legislative veto. Ma major rule is proposed and a single House of Congress votes *not* to authorize it, the rule is defeated. The same would have been true under the one-house veto scheme of *Chadha.* However, these superficial similarities do not have any constitutional consequence. The same thing could be said of *any* bill proposed for Congress's consideration: the requirement of bicameralism means that both the House and the Senate must agree to make new law, so a single House has complete power to prevent a bill from becoming law. *Chadha* itself cautioned against "analogiz[ing] the effect of the [legislative veto] to the failure of one house to vote *affirmatively on a* private bill"; the latter complies with the Constitution's requirements, while the former does not.[42]

In fact, the REINS Act would not be the first time that Congress has required specific legislation of this form. The Reorganization Act[43] provides that a reorganization plan proposed by the President will take effect only if Congress *approves* a confirmatory joint resolution through a fast-track procedure within 90 days.[44] This is precisely the same mechanism used by the REINS Act: executive proposal and legislative enactment. Congress has previously used similar mechanisms for fast-track trade authority[45] and adoption of Presidential recommendations on Congressional pay.[46] Because these procedures rely on legislation, rather than extralegislative acts, they are entirely consistent with the Constitution.

3. The Houses of Congress Have Power to Create Fast-Track Procedures

The final aspect of the bill is the fast-track procedure it creates for enacting a joint resolution to approve a major rule. This aspect, too, *falls* comfortably within *the* powers of the two Houses of Congress. Article I, Section 5, Clause 2 states that "[e]ach House may determine the Rules of its Proceedings." As is described in section 802(h)(1) of the bill, in passing the REINS Act each House would be using its own internal rule-making powers to adopt the fast-track procedure. That adoption is made conditional on the Act's ultimate passage, through approval by the other House and presentment to the President. Under the Constitution, each House has the right to determine its own procedures, as well as to condition its adoption of those procedures on the passage of confirmatory legislation.

The two Houses of Congress have adopted internal rules jointly in the form of statutes since the earliest days of the Republic. In fact, the very first statute enacted by the First Congress on June 1, 1789, addressed the procedures for administering oaths in the *House* and Senate, a matter that was within the power of each House to determine independently.[47] As the Supreme Court has recognized, the decisions of the First Congress provide "contemporaneous and weighty evidence of the Constitution's meaning since many of the Members of the First Congress had taken part in *framing* that instrument."[48] And as noted above, Congress has exercised the power to create a fast-track procedure many times since then, including in the existing text of the CRA.

Moreover, the REINS Act does not restrict either House's constitutional power to determine "the Rules of its Proceedings" in the future. Instead, section 802(h)(2) of the bill "recogni[zes] * * * the constitutional right *of either* House to change the *rules"* of its internal procedures "at any time." Even after the bill's passage, each House retains the authority to amend its rules through the normal procedure. But the REINS Act's procedures would remain fully valid until amended, and would serve both as a common reference point and as a useful means of coordination between the Houses.

B. The Reins Act Would Help to Enforce the Constitution's Separation of Powers

In requiring specific Congressional approval for major agency rules, the REINS Act is not merely itself consistent with the requirements of the Constitution. Rather, the bill would also help ensure that the rules themselves are consistent with the Constitution's separation of powers. In particular, the bill would make elected officials accountable for the work of unelected bureaucrats — enforcing Article I's exclusive vesting of legislative power in Congress, and Article II's exclusive vesting of executive power in the President.

I. The Reins Act Would Enforce the Vesting of Legislative Power in Congress

By requiring major agency rules to receive Congressional approval, the REINS Act would significantly assist in enforcing the non-delegation doctrine. That doctrine stands for the simple principle that under our Constitution, the lawmaking function belongs to Congress, and may not be conveyed to another branch or entity."[49] Article I, Section 1 of the Constitution states that *"[a]ll* legislative Powers herein granted shall be vested in a Congress of the United States." The text "permits no delegation of those powers" to an administrative agency.[50]

Of course Congress may, in the exercise of its powers under the Necessary and Proper Clause, lay down a "general provision" by enactment and then require the Executive Branch to "fill up the details."[51] But as Chief Justice John Marshall wrote, Congress may not simply hand over to the bureaucracy crucial policy decisions on "those important subjects, which must be entirely regulated by the legislature itself."[52]

Since Chief Justice Marshall wrote, courts have struggled to draw a line between the questions that Congress may decide and those that may be delegated to administrative agencies. Under current law, a delegation of regulatory authority will be upheld so long as it "fay[sl down * * * an *intelligible principle* to which the person or body authorized * * * is directed to conform."[53]

But the "intelligible principle" standard has done little to constrain the discretion of administrative agencies. Instead, the courts have essentially abandoned the field of enforcing the nondelegation doctrine — unanimously upholding, for example, a statute authorizing any air quality standards "requisite to protect the public health."[54] No less an authority than Cass Sunstein — now head of the Office of Information and Regulatory Affairs — has questioned whether the Occupational Safety and Health Act is constitutional, because it delegates the power to implement any standard that is "reasonably necessary or appropriate to provide safe or healthful employment and places of employment."[55] This acceptance of vague legislation and unrestricted agency authority has led some to question whether *any* statute — even one requiring *agencies* to promote "goodness and niceness" and authorizing them to regulate accordingly — could be invalidated today on non-delegation grounds.[56]

The REINS Act would not solve the non-delegation problem entirely. As section 802(g) of the bill makes clear, the approval vote only satisfies one of many conditions that a regulation must meet in order to have legal effect. If the rule is a product of an unconstitutional delegation of power, the approval vote will not cure that flaw.

What the REINS Act will do, however, is prevent some of the greatest dangers of excessive delegation, by ensuring that Congress remains accountable for the rules that are promulgated in its name. In public life, as Alexander Hamilton knew, "[i]t often becomes impossible, amidst mutual accusations, to determine *on whom* the blame or the punishment *of* a pernicious measure, or series of pernicious measures, ought really to fall. It is shifted from one to another with so much dexterity, and under such plausible appearances, that the public opinion is left in suspense about the real author."[57] When legislators delegate broad authority to a *faceless* bureaucracy, they can take credit for someone else's success and shift responsibility for someone else's failure. That is a recipe for over-regulation.

By contrast, under the REINS Act, every time a new rule takes effect the public will know which of their representatives deserve the praise or blame — and how to respond on Election Day. Even if Congress has improperly delegated its decision-*making* power to unelected officials, Members of Congress will still have to take individual responsibility for the decisions those officials make. That increased accountability does a great deal to restore the Constitution's vision of legislative power being vested in a Congress responsible to the people. "The Framers recognized that, in the long term, structural protections against abuse of power were critical to preserving liberty."[58]

The REINS Act properly applies its highest level of scrutiny to major rules with a major impact on Americans' lives. That kind of rule should not just be approved by bureaucrats with civil service protections, but by representatives who are regularly held accountable at the voting booth. In this way, it follows Chief Justice Marshall's distinction between "those important subjects, which must be entirely regulated by the legislature itself, from those of less interest, in which a general provision may be made, and power given to those who are to act under such general provisions to fill up the details."[59] Under the REINS Act, the "important subjects" will never be regulated without the specific authorization *of* the people's elected representatives.

2. The REINS Act Would Enforce the Vesting of Executive Power in the President

The REINS Act would also help to enforce the Executive Vesting Clause of the Constitution, which vests the Federal Government's executive powers in the President of the United States. Section 804(1) of the bill applies its requirements to rules from any administrative "agency," as that term is used in 5 U.S.C. § 551(1). That includes agencies staffed by executive officers whose tenure is said to be protected from Presidential removal. For example, according to statute, the President can remove members of the Federal Trade Commission only "for inefficiency, neglect of duty, or malfeasance *in* office"[60] — and not simply because he disagrees with their policies or regulatory priorities. Without the ability to fire these officers, the President cannot control what their *agencies* do — even though they wield executive power, and even though the Constitution provides that "[t]he executive Power shall be vested in a President of the United States of America."[61]

Just as members of Congress may avoid blame for the actions of bureaucracies they empower, the President is currently able to escape responsibility for the actions of independent officers who ostensibly exercise power on his behalf. When tenured officials at the FTC, the Consumer Product Safety Commission, the Federal Energy Regulatory Commission, or the National Labor Relations Board issue wide-ranging new regulations affecting millions of Americans, there is little the President can do to stop them. And because these officials do not stand for election, the voting public can do even less. As the Supreme Court recently explained, "Mlle growth of the Executive Branch, which now wields vast power and touches almost every aspect of daily life, heightens the concern that it may slip from the Executive's control, and thus from that of the people."[62]

The REINS Act would not interfere with the statutory tenure protections of independent agency officials. But it would do a great deal to restore the President's constitutional responsibility for the actions of the Executive Branch. Under the REINS Act, major rules enacted by independent agencies — no less than major rules enacted by agencies subject to the President's control — would have to be authorized by legislation, passed by both Houses of Congress, and presented to the *President for his* review. If the President disapproves of a rule, he can veto its authorizing resolution; if he endorses it, he can allow it to take effect. Either way, the President is forced to take ownership of the independent agency's action and will be held accountable by the people for his choice.

Under our Constitution, the President "cannot delegate *ultimate* responsibility or the active obligation to supervise that goes with it," because Article II "makes a single President responsible for the actions of the Executive Branch."[63] The REINS Act enhances that *responsibility* by forcing the President to decide whether every major regulation, even those proposed by officers with statutory tenure protections, will go into effect. This mandate preserves the Constitution's "require[mentj that a President chosen by the entire Nation oversee the execution of the laws."[64]

In conclusion, I urge the Committee to continue its examination of the regulatory procedure — especially given the enormous burden that Federal regulations place on the private economy. In addition, I recommend the adoption of the REINS Act as an excellent *means* of ensuring greater accountability for regulatory policy and to strengthen the constitutionality of the regulatory process. In the meantime, I would urge Members of Congress to make full use of Congress's oversight powers, the power of the purse, and the Congressional Review Act to put the brakes on new, costly regulations and in so doing increase economic growth and job creation. Thank you very much.

End Notes

[1] As I say the views expressed in this testimony are my own. I would like to thank my colleague, Stephen E. Sachs, for his excellent constitutional and legal analysis and help in drafting this testimony.

[2] Susan E. Dudley, *President Obama's Executive Order: improving Regulations and Regulatory Review*, Regulatory Policy Commentary, The George Washington University Regulatory Studies Center, at 1 (Jan. 18, 2011), http://www.regulatorystudies.gwu.edu/images commentary/20110118_reg_eo.pdf,

[3] Nicole V. Crain & W. Mark Crain, *The Impact of Regulatory Costs on Small Firms*, Small Business Admin., Small Business Research Summary No. 371 (Sept. 2010), http://archive.sba.goviadvoiresearchirs371.pdf.

[4] *See* Council of Economic Advisers, Economic Report of the President tbl. B-81, at 426 (2010), http://www.gpoaccess.gov/eop/2010/ 2010_erp.pdf; *see also* James L. Gattuso et al., *Red Tape Rising*, Heritage Foundation Backgrounder No. 2482, at 1 (Oct. 26, 2010), http://thf_media.s3.amazonaws.com/2010/pdf/bg2482.pdf.

[5] Dudley, *supra* note 2, at 2. Gattuso et al., *supra* note 4, at 2.

[7] *See generally* Gattuso et al., *supra* note 4, at 3 (describing cost data).

[8] This rule represents the first time that "greenhouse gas" emissions performance was applied in a regulatory context for a nationwide program.

[9] *See* Light-Duty Vehicle Greenhouse Gas Emission Standards and Corporate Average Fuel Economy Standards; Final Rule, 75 Fed. Reg. 25,324 (May 7, 2010).

[10] Regulation of Fuels and Fuel Additives: Changes to Renewable Fuel Standard Program, 75 Fed. Reg. 14,670 (March 26, 2010). The EPA projects several indirect costs in its Regulatory Impact Analysis, including food increases of $10 per person per year, or $3.6 billion, by 2022. This was not included in the total by Gattuso et al. *See* Gattuso et al., *supra* note 4, at 3 n.8; *see also* EPA, Renewable Fuel Standard Program (RFS2) Regulatory Impact Analysis 5 (Feb. 2010), http://www.epa.gov/otaq/renewablefuels/420r10006.pdf.

[11] Energy Conservation Program: Energy Conservation Standards for Residential Water Heaters, Direct Heating Equipment, and Pool Heaters, 75 Fed. Reg. 20,112 (Apr. 16, 2010).

[12] Gattuso et al., *supra note* 4, at 5; Davis Polk & Wardwell, LLP, Summary of the Dodd-Frank Wall Street Reform and Consumer Protection Act, Enacted into Law on July 21, 2010, (July 21, 2010), http://www.davispolk.com/files/Publication/7084f9fe-6580-413bb870-b7c 025ed2ecf/Presentation/PublicationAttachment/1d4495c7- Obe0-4e9a-ba774786fb90464a /070910_FinancialReform_ Summary.pdf (October 21, 2010).

[13] Cong. Res. Serv., Deadlines for the Secretary of Health and Human Services in the Patient Protection and Affordable Care Act from Enactment to January 1,2011 (October 1,2010), at http://coburn.senate.gov/public/index.cfm?a=Files.Serve&Fileid=54103bf6-ae3a-47be-916e-72548ba34b5b.

[14] In the Matter of Preserving the Open Internet Broadband Industry Practices, FCC GN Docket No. 09-191, WC Docket No. 07-52, Statement of Commissioner Robert McDowell, Dec. 21, 2010.

[15] *See, e.g.*, Reed Garfield, Smothering Economic Growth One Regulation at a Time, Joint Economic Committee Report (June 1996), http://www.house.govijeckost-goviregs/cost Benjamin Bridgman et al., *Does Regulation Reduce Productivity? Evidence From Regulation of the U.S. Beet-Sugar Manufacturing Industry During the Sugar Acts, 1934-74*, Fed. Reserve Bank of Minneapolis, Res. Dep't Staff Report 38 (Apr. 2007),

http://www.minneapolisfed.oreresearch/SR/SR389.pdf; Wayne B. Gray, *The Cost of Regulation: OSHA, EPA and the Productivity Slowdown,* 77 Am. Econ. Rev. 998 (1987).

16

[16] Crain & Crain, *supra* note 3, at 1.

17 A major rule is defined as "any rule that the Administrator of the Office of Information and Regulatory Affairs of the Office of *Management* and *Budget finds has resulted in or* is likely to result in — an annual effect on the economy of $100,000,000 or more; a major increase in costs or prices for consumers, individual industries, Federal, State, or local government agencies, or geographic regions; or significant adverse effects on competition, employment, investment, productivity, innovation, or on the ability of United States-based enterprises to compete with foreign-based enterprises in domestic and export markets."

[18] 5 U.S.C. § 801(a)(1)(A).

[19] Curtis W. Copeland, Cong. Res. Serv., Congressional Review Act: Rules Not Submitted to GAO and Congress 10 (Dec. 29, 2009),
http:// assets *see also* Sean D. Croston, *Congress and the Courts Close Their Eyes,* 62 Admin. L Rev. 907 (2010).

[20] *Via Christi Regional Med. Ctr., Inc. v. Leavitt,* 509 F.3d 1259, 1271 n.11. (10th Cir. 2007); *see also Montanans. For Multiple Use v. Barbouletos,* 568 F.3d 225, 229 (D.C. Cir. 2009).

[21] All section references are to the sections of title 5, United States Code, that would be amended by the REINS Act.

[22] *See* Stephen Breyer, *The Thomas F. Ryan Lecture: The Legislative Veto After* Chadha, 72 Geo. L.J. 785, 789 (1984).

[23] Art. I, § 8, cl. 18.

[24] *Free Enterprise Fund v. Public Company Accounting Oversight Board (PCAOB),* 130 S. Ct. 3138, 3155 (2010).

[25] *La. Pub. Serv. Comm'n v. FCC,* 476 U.S. 355, 374 (1986).

[26] *CAB v. Delta Air Lines, Inc.,* 367 U.S. 316, 322 (1961).

[27] *See* 5 U.S.C. §§ 553, 706(2)(A).

[28] *See, e.g., Whitman v. Am. Trucking Asens,* 531. U.S. 457, 465-67 (2001) (construing section 109(b)(1) of the Clean Air Act to forbid such considerations, while other sections of the same Act require them).

[29] *Bowen v. Georgetown Univ. Hosp.,* 488 U.S. 204, 208 (1988).

[30] *INS v. Chadha,* 462 U.S. 919, 952 (1983).

[31] Art. I, §1.

[32] Art. 1, § 7, cl. 2-3.

[33] 462 U.S. 919. [34] *Id. at* 954.

[35] *Id.* at 955.

[35] *Id.* at 946, 948.

[37] 478 U.S. 714, 733-34 (1986).

[38] *Bowsher,* 478 U.S. at 733-34.

[39] Breyer, *supra* note 22, at 789.

[40] *Id.* at 793.

[41] *Id.*

[42] 462 U.S. at 958 n.23 (internal quotation marks omitted).

[43] 5 U.S.C. § 901 *et seq.*

[44] *See §§* 906(a), 909-912.

[45] *See, e.g.,* 19 U.S.C. § 2191.

[46] *See, e.g.,* 2 U.S.C. § 359.

[47] Act of June 1, 1789, ch. 1, § 2, 1 Stat. 23, 23 (codified as amended at 2 U.S.C. §§ 21-25).
[48] *Bowsher,* 478 U.S. at 723-24.
[49] *Loving v. United States,* 517 U.S. 748, 758 (1996) (citation omitted).
[50] *American Trucking,* 531 U.S. at 472.
[51] *Wayman v. Southard,* 23 U.S. (10 Wheat.) 1, 23 (1825).
[52] *id.*
[53] *American Trucking,* 531 U.S. at 472 (emphasis added; internal quotation marks omitted).
[54] *Af77. Trucking,* 531 U.S. *at 473.*
[55] 29 U.S.C. § 652(8). *See* Cass R. Sunstein, *Is OSHA Unconstitutional?,* 94 Va. L. Rev. 1407 (2008).
[56] Gary Lawson, *Delegation and Original Meaning,* 88 Va. L. Rev. 327, 345, 355 (2002).
[57] The Federalist No. 70.
[58] *Bowsher, 478 U.S. at* 730.
[59] *Wayman,* 23 U.S. at 23.
[60] 15 U.S.C. § 41.
[61] Art. II, § 1, cf. 1.
[62] *PCAOB,* 130 S. Ct. at 3156.
[63] *Clinton v. Jones,* 520 U. 5. 681, 712-13 (1997) (Breyer, J., concurring in judgment).
[64] *PCAOB,* 130 S. Ct. at 3155-56.

In: Federal Government and the REINS Act ISBN: 978-1-62100-346-5
Editors: L. Matthews and J. Fanning

Chapter 3

PREPARED STATEMENT OF JONATHAN H. ADLER BEFORE THE SUBCOMMITTEE ON COURTS, COMMERCIAL AND ADMINISTRATIVE LAW COMMITTEE ON THE JUDICIARY U.S. HOUSE OF REPRESENTATIVES, HEARING ON " THE REINS ACT - PROMOTING JOBS AND EXPANDING FREEDOM BY REDUCING NEEDLESS REGULATION*

Jonathan Adler
Professor of Law
Director, Center for Business and Regulation
11075 East Boulevard Cleveland, Ohio 44137-7148
Phone 216-368-2535
Fax 216-368-2086
E-mail jha5@case.edu
www.law.case.edu

* This is an edited, reformatted and augmented version of statement given by Jonathan H. Adler before the Subcommittee on Courts, Commercial and Administrative Law Committee on the Judiciary U.S. House of Representatives, Hearing on "The REINS Act - Promoting Jobs and Expanding Freedom by Reducing Needless Regulation on January 24, 2011.

Thank you, Mr. Chairman and members of this subcommittee, for the invitation to testify on the REINS Act. My name is Jonathan H. Adler, and I am a Professor of Law and Director of the Center for Business Law and Regulation at the Case Western Reserve University School of Law, where I teach various courses in administrative, environmental and constitutional law. I appreciate the opportunity to appear before this subcommittee to discuss measures Congress may take to exercise greater control over the cost and reach of federal regulations and enhance political accountability.

THE NEED FOR REGULATORY ACCOUNTABILITY

Over the past several decades, the scope, reach and cost of federal regulations have increased dramatically. From the 1950s through the 2000s, the amount of federal regulatory activity, as measured by pages in the *Federal Register*, has increased more than six-fold. In the 1950s, federal agencies published an average of just under 11,000 pages in the *Federal Register* per year. From 2001-2009, federal agencies averaged over 73,000 pages per year.[1] In 2010, the *Federal Register* contained over 82,000 pages, the greatest number in over a decade and the third highest total in our nation's history. The number of new final rules each year has declined, but federal regulations are still adopted at a rapid pace. In 2008 and 2009 federal regulatory agencies adopted 3,830 and 3,503 final rules, respectively.[2] These rules cover everything from greenhouse gas emission reporting and proxy disclosures to electronic fund transfers and the energy and water use of home appliances. Substantially more regulation is on the way. By some estimates, the Wall Street Reform and Consumer Protection Act alone will require over 200 federal rulemakings.[3]

The growth of federal regulation has imposed significant costs on American business and consumers. According to recent estimates, the total cost of federal regulation exceeds $1.1 trillion dollars per year.[4] This is substantially more than the total amount of individual income taxes paid by Americans each year.[5] Insofar as they impose substantial costs, regulations are like a hidden tax. Just like taxes, regulations may be necessary to address public ills or to provide important public benefits, but this does not mean they are free. The fact that regulations, like taxes, can both impose substantial costs and generate substantial benefits makes it that much more important that there be political accountability for federal regulatory decisions.

This dramatic increase in the scope of federal regulation has been facilitated by the practice of delegating substantial amounts of regulatory authority and policy discretion to federal regulatory agencies. Federal regulatory agencies have no inherent powers. Article I, section 1 of the Constitution vests all legislative power in the Congress. Federal agencies only have the power to adopt rules governing private conduct if such power has been delegated to them through a valid statutory enactment. As the Supreme Court has explained, "It is axiomatic that an administrative agency's power to promulgate legislative regulation is limited to the authority delegated by Congress."[6]

Over the course of the twentieth century, Congress has delegated ever greater amounts of regulatory authority to an ever-expanding array of federal agencies. Congress has often had good reasons for this. The economic, environmental and other problems Congress sought to address were complicated and often necessitated careful study and analysis. Delegation of regulatory authority to expert agencies with the time and expertise to focus on specific problems was a way to ensure that federal regulations were adopted to address the nuances and particulars of specific problems.

Delegation may have been expedient, or even necessary, but it has also had a cost. The delegation of broad and far-reaching regulatory authority has undermined political accountability for regulatory decisions and has allowed for regulatory agencies to adopt policies that did not always align with Congressional intent or contemporary priorities. When Congress delegates broad regulatory authority to executive or independent agencies, it inevitably loses some degree of control over how that authority is exercised. If a federal agency is instructed to adopt measures that serve the public interest or control a given environmental problem as far as is practicable, the federal agency retains substantial discretion to determine what sorts of measures should be adopted and at what cost. Judicial review serves to ensure that agencies play by the rules set out by Congress – that agencies provide adequate notice and opportunity for public participation, provide sufficient explanations for the rules they adopt, observe the limits of their regulatory jurisdiction, and so on. Yet judicial review does not delve into the policy choices agencies make – nor should it. Whether a given agency is following the best course is ultimately a decision for the political branches.

In principle, the delegation doctrine ensures that Congress remains responsible for the major policy judgments that drive regulatory decisions.[7] In practice, however, the doctrine does not serve this purpose very well. Under existing precedent, Congress need only provide federal agencies with an "intelligible principle" to guide regulatory initiatives, and it does not take much to satisfy this standard. Any broad statement of policy will do, leaving federal agencies with tremendous amounts of discretion in how they exercise their regulatory power, including whether to exercise such power at all and even when, if ever, to change their mind. Under existing doctrine agencies are free to reverse course and overturn prior policies without any meaningful input from Congress.

The difficulty of ensuring that agencies remain accountable for their policy choices is magnified by time. Agencies today continue to exercise authority granted decades ago. To take a current example, the Environmental Protection Agency is in the midst of implementing a series of regulations governing the emission of greenhouse gases from mobile and stationary sources. These regulations are intended to address an important environmental concern and will have a tremendous effect on the American economy as they threaten to impact literally hundreds of thousands of facilities across the nation. The EPA's authority for these regulations is a statute passed by Congress, the Clean Air Act. Yet there is no indication that the current or recently concluded Congresses support the EPA's actions.

The Clean Air Act's basic architecture was enacted in 1970. Key provisions were added in 1977 and 1990, and the Act has not been amended to any significant degree in over twenty years. According to the EPA, these decades-olds provisions authorize (if not compel) it to regulate greenhouse gas emissions from cars and trucks, utilities, factories, and other sources. According to the EPA, the legislative grant of authority it received decades ago drives its decisions today, even though Congress was not at all focused on global warming when the relevant provisions of the Clean Air Act were adopted, relatively few members of Congress who voted for the Clean Air Act remain in Congress today, and Congress has never taken any action to affirmatively approve such regulation in the years since the Act was adopted or amended. Although the EPA is exercising authority ostensibly delegated by Congress, Congress is not politically accountable for the EPA's actions. Further, insofar as some maintain that the EPA's actions are based upon a misreading of Congressional intent, it is difficult for Congress to correct the agency's course without going through the lengthy and time-consuming process of amending statutes that are on the books.

The above is hardly an isolated example. Numerous federal agencies continue to exercise substantial regulatory authority under old and often outdated statutes. Though the statutes were passed by Congress, and Congress is ultimately responsible for the power these agencies wield, Congress is not particularly accountable for how agencies today exercise power granted years ago. Agency authority, once granted, is difficult to modify or repeal. Drafting and adopting new legislation to revise existing agency authority is a laborious process not well suited to active agency oversight and control.

Executive oversight of federal agencies is certainly important, but it is no substitute for legislative oversight and control. Regulatory agencies get their power from Congress, not the President, and it is ultimately Congress' responsibility to make sure that this responsibility is exercised properly. Executive Branch review to ensure agency rules are cost-effective or line-up with Presidential priorities does not mean that such initiatives are supported by Congress, or the American people. The Congress, and the House of Representatives in particular, is more responsive to the people – and therefore more politically accountable – than the executive branch. Further, there are many agencies – so-called independent agencies – that are not subject to meaningful executive oversight, making the need for legislative oversight and control that much greater.

Executive oversight also does not ensure that agencies are acting in accord with Congressional intent. Indeed, Executive Branch and independent agencies often seek to evade legislative oversight and control. With increasing frequency the executive branch has sought to achieve through regulation what it has been unable to achieve through legislation. After failing to get Congress to pass desired legislation, each of the last two administrations resorted to the administrative process to achieve their desired policy ends. Such end-runs around the legislative process appear to be on the rise, and the deferential nature of judicial review of agency action has hardly slowed such efforts. As a consequence the Executive Branch and independent agencies increasingly escape legislative control and political accountability for their actions.

Past Efforts to Enhance Legislative Control and Political Accountability

Over the years Congress has adopted various reforms aimed at restoring political accountability, disciplining federal agencies, and ensuring that federal regulatory policy is responsive to contemporary legislative priorities, without sacrificing the practical benefits of delegation. Indeed, legislative oversight and review has, in many respects, facilitated greater delegations of regulatory authority, as Congress may be more comfortable delegating substantial amounts of power if it is assured that it retains a degree of oversight and control.[8] While well-intentioned, these efforts have been largely unsuccessful.

In the mid-twentieth century, Congress attempted to control administrative agency decision-making through the adoption of legislative veto provisions. Between the 1930s and 1980s, Congress enacted legislative veto provisions into nearly 300 statutes. These provisions enabled Congress to delegate broad legislative-like authority to administrative agencies while retaining the unilateral authority to overturn administrative decisions through legislative action, but without Presidential assent or a veto-proof majority.

A typical legislative veto provision was contained in the Immigration and Nationality Act, which authorized either House of Congress to invalidate a decision by the Attorney General to allow an otherwise deportable alien to remain in the United States with a simple resolution passed by majority vote. By allowing either House to override an agency decision, the legislative veto provisions effectively required concurrent agreement by the President and both houses of Congress for an agency decision could take effect, for dissent by either the Senate or the House of Representatives was enough to veto the action. Such provisions were popular, but they were not long-lived.

In 1983 the Supreme Court invalidated unicameral legislative vetoes in *Immigration and Nationalization Service v. Chadha*.[9] The Court held (correctly in my view) that it was unconstitutional for a single house of Congress to overturn an administrative action taken pursuant to a valid grant of legislative authority. Overturning an administrative action was, in effect, a legislative act. Under Article I of the Constitution, legislative acts require bicameralism and presentment – the concurrence of both Houses of Congress and presentation before the President for his signature or veto, the latter of which could be overturned by super-majorities in both legislative chambers.

A more recent example of legislative efforts to control the regulatory process and increase political accountability was the Congressional Review Act, enacted in 1996. The CRA created an expedited process for consideration of joint resolutions to overturn regulations of which Congress disapproved. Unlike the unicameral vetoes voided in *Chadha*, resolutions of disapproval under the CRA must be passed by both Houses and presented to the President for signature. In effect, the CRA created a framework for Congress to enact new laws to overturn or correct administrative implementation of previously enacted laws.

The CRA created a mechanism whereby Congress could, at its own initiative, act to overturn administrative action. Yet the CRA has not been particularly effective – and this should not surprise. There is tremendous inertia within the legislative process, and if Congress is required to take the initiative to overturn an unjustified or excessive regulation, it is unlikely to happen. Other priorities compete for legislators' time and attention, and members of Congress are not always eager to cast a vote for or against a controversial or high-profile regulation. As a consequence, the CRA has only been used once, and it is not widely considered to have disciplined agency action or increased Congressional accountability for regulatory initiatives. One particular problem is that the CRA effectively requires a super-majority in Congress to overturn an administrative action as, in all likelihood, a sitting President will veto a resolution overturning one of his own administration's regulatory initiatives.[10] Only those rules adopted near the end of a President's term are particularly vulnerable to CRA repeal, and the Executive can reduce the vulnerability of regulations to CRA review by ensuring new rules are not issued at the tail end of a presidential term.

THE REINS ACT

The Regulations from the Executive in Needs of Scrutiny (REINS) Act offers a promising mechanism for disciplining federal regulatory agencies and enhancing Congressional accountability for federal regulations. Requiring Congressional approval before economically significant rules may take effect ensures that Congress takes responsibility for major economic policy decisions of the sort that are embodied in the most significant federal regulations. Adopting an expedited legislative process, much like that which is used for fast-track trade authority, ensures transparency and prevents a Congressional review process from unduly delaying needed regulatory initiatives. Such an approach can enhance political accountability without sacrificing the benefits of agency expertise and specialization.

As then-judge Stephen Breyer explained in a 1984 lecture, a congressional authorization requirement of this sort could replicate the function of the legislative veto invalidated in *Chadha* without the veto's constitutional infirmity.[11] By observing the formal requirements for legislation in Article I, he explained, congressional oversight of agency activity could be maintained without violating constitutional principles of separation of powers. In addition, unlike the legislative veto, requiring Congressional approval for the adoption of new regulatory initiatives "imposes on Congress a degree of visible responsibility" for new regulatory initiatives.[12]

The presentment clause in Article I, section 7 of the Constitution provides that, for a bill to become law, it must be passed by a majority of both the House and Senate and signed into law by the President or, if vetoed by the President, repassed by two-thirds majorities in each house. It further provides that "[e]very Order, Resolution, or Vote to which the Concurrence of the Senate and House of Representatives may be necessary . . . shall be presented to the President of the United States" for his signature or veto. The REINS Act complies with this requirement, and is therefore constitutional.[13] Just like any other bill, a Joint Resolution requires the approval of both houses of Congress and is presented to the President.[14]

In some respects the REINS Act is more limited than Breyer's suggested proposal for congressional resolutions of approval for regulatory measures or the unicameral legislative vetoes at issue in *Chadha*, as the REINS Act would only require congressional approval for so-called "major rules." The unicameral legislative veto often operated as a replacement for targeted "private bills" affecting the interests of a few. [15] By contrast, those regulations subject to the REINS Act would, by definition, be only those that have broader impacts on large segments of the country, if not the nation as a whole. Only those rules deemed to be "economically significant" are covered, and such rules are a small, but important, portion of federal regulatory activity. From 1998-2007, the number of major rules promulgated by federal administrative agencies ranged between fifty and eighty per year.[16]

One objection to requiring Congressional approval before major rules may take effect is that regulatory initiatives could be subject to procedural delays, particularly in the Senate, and that such a requirement would make it too easy for a determined minority or special interest group to block desirable regulations. The REINS Act seeks to address this concern by creating an expedited process for consideration of a joint resolution approving major rules in both the House and Senate. A joint resolution of approval is automatically introduced into both houses within three days of a federal agency's submission of a major rule to Congress, and legislative committees have only fifteen days to consider the resolution before it is automatically discharged. Debate on the resolution is limited, and other motions that could postpone or prolong debate are prohibited, as are amendments to the rule, so as to ensure that each House votes up-or-down on the resolution shortly after it is presented to Congress. Similar processes are used in other contexts, as with fast-track trade negotiation authority, so there is no reason why such a process could not be used here as well.

The REINS Act provides a means of curbing excessive or unwarranted regulation, but it is not an obstacle to needed regulatory measures supported by the public. If agencies are generally discharging their obligations in a sensible manner, REINS Act-type controls will have little effect. If the public believes that more regulations are necessary, or supports regulatory initiatives of a particular type, requiring a resolution of Congressional approval will not stand in the way. Indeed, it would enhance the legitimacy of those regulations Congress approves by making clear that such initiatives command the support of both the legislative and executive branches. Above all else, the REINS Act provides a means of enhancing political accountability for regulatory policy.

* * *

Mister Chairman and members of this committee, I recognize the importance of these issues to you and your constituents. I hope that my perspective has been helpful to you, and I will seek to answer any additional questions you might have. Thank you.

End Notes

[1] See Clyde Wayne Crews, Ten Thousand Commandments: A Snapshot of the Federal Regulatory State (2010 edition), at 16.

[2] Id. at 38.

[3] See "Summary of the Dodd–Frank Wall Street Reform and Consumer Protection Act, Enacted into Law on July 21, 2010," Davis Polk & Wardwell, LLP, July 21, 2010, available at http://www.davispolk.com/files/Publication/7084f9fe-6580-413b-b870-b7c025ed2ecf/Presentation/PublicationAttachment/1d4495c7-0be0-4e9a-ba77-f786fb90464a/070910_Financial_Reform_Summary.pdf

[4] See Crews at 6.

[5] Id. at 9-10.

[6] Bowen v. Georgetown University Hospital, 488 U.S. 204 208 (1988); see also Louisiana Public Service Commission v. FCC, 476 U.S. 355, 374 (1986)("an agency literally has no power to act . . . unless and until Congress confers power upon it.").

[7] See Loving v. United States, 517 U.S. 748, 757 (1996) ("The delegation doctrine [was] developed to prevent Congress from forsaking its duties"); see also Industrial Union Dept., AFL-CIO v. American Petroleum Institute, 448 U.S. 607, 685 (1980) (Rehnquist, J., concurring) (the doctrine ensures that "important choices of social policy are made by Congress, the branch of our Government most responsible to the popular will.").

[8] See INS v. Chadha, 462 U.S. 919, 974 (1983) ("the Executive has . . . [generally] agreed to legislative review as the price for a broad delegation of authority") (White, J. dissenting). See also Michael Herz, The Legislative Veto in Times of Political Reversal: Chadha and the 104th Congress, 14 CONSTITUTIONAL COMMENTARY 319, 324 (1997) (noting that the

legislative veto was developed "as a means of allowing massive concessions of authority to the executive" by ensuring Congress would retain the ability to review and control such delegations).

[9] 462 U.S. 919 (1983).

[10] See Nick Smith, Restoration of Congressional Authority and Responsibility Over the Regulatory Process, 33 HARVARD JOURNAL ON LEGISLATION 323, 326 (1996); see also Michael Herz, The Legislative Veto in Times of Political Reversal: Chadha and the 104th Congress, 14 CONSTITUTIONAL COMMENTARY 319, 323 (1997) ("Requiring presidential approval (or a two-thirds majority to override) is hardly a formality.").

[11] See Stephen Breyer, The Legislative Veto After Chadha, 72 GEORGETOWN LAW JOURNAL 785, 793-96 (1984).

[12] Breyer, at 794.

[13] See also Laurence H. Tribe, The Legislative Veto Decision: A Law by Any Other Name? 21 HARVARD JOURNAL ON LEGISLATION 1, 19 (1984) (noting that a congressional approval requirement for agency regulations would be constitutional).

[14] The only exception to this rule is a Joint Resolution used to propose a constitutional amendment. Such a resolution is instead submitted to the states for ratification. See http://www.senate.gov/reference/glossary_term/joint_resolution.htm.

[15] In Chadha, the House of Representatives voted to overturn six of 340 cases in which the Attorney General had concluded an otherwise deportable alien should be allowed to remain in the United States.

[16] Crews, at 28.

In: Federal Government and the REINS Act ISBN: 978-1-62100-346-5
Editors: L. Matthews and J. Fanning

Chapter 4

STATEMENT OF SALLY KATZEN BEFORE THE SUBCOMMITTEE ON COURTS, COMMERCIAL AND ADMINISTRATIVE LAW OF THE HOUSE COMMITTEE ON THE JUDICIARY, HEARING ON "THE REINS ACT - PROMOTING JOBS AND EXPANDING FREEDOM BY REDUCING NEEDLESS REGULATIONS"*

Chairman Coble, Ranking Member Cohen, Members of the Subcommittee. Thank you for inviting me to testify today. I have been privileged to appear before this Committee on a number of occasions, both as a government official and as a private citizen.

As you know, I served as the Administrator of the Office of Information and Regulatory Affairs (OIRA) at the Office of Management and Budget (OMB) for the first five years of the Clinton Administration, then as the Deputy Assistant to the President for Economic Policy and Deputy Director of the National Economic Council, and then as the Deputy Director for Management of OMB. After leaving government service in January 2001, I taught administrative law courses at the University of Michigan Law School, George Washington University Law School, George Mason University Law

---

* This is an edited, reformatted and augmented version of statement given by Sally Katzen before the Subcommittee on Courts, Commercial and Administrative Law of the House Committee on the Judiciary, Hearing on "The REINS Act - Promoting Jobs and Expanding Freedom by Reducing Needless Regulations" on January 24, 2011.

School, and the University of Pennsylvania Law School, and I also taught American Government courses to undergraduates at Smith College, Johns Hopkins University, and the University of Michigan in Washington Program; this semester, I am teaching a seminar in advanced administrative law at NYU Law School and am a Senior Adviser at the Podesta Group. Before entering government service, I was the Chair of the ABA Section on Administrative Law and Regulatory Practice (1988-89), and during my government service, I was the Vice Chair (and Acting Chair) of the Administrative Conference of the United States (ACUS). I have written articles for scholarly publications and have frequently been asked to speak on administrative law in general and rulemaking in particular.

The subject of today's hearing is OMB's Report to Congress does include data on benefits, and the numbers are striking: according to OMB, the benefits from the regulations issued during the ten-year period ranged from \$128 billion to \$616 billion. Therefore, even if one uses OMB's highest estimate of costs and its lowest estimate of benefits, the regulations issued over the past ten years have produced net benefits of \$73 billion to our society. This cannot be dismissed as a partisan report by the current administration, because OMB issued reports with similar results (benefits greatly exceeding costs) throughout the George W. Bush Administration (e.g., for FY 1998-2008, major regulations cost between \$51 and \$60 billion, with benefits estimated to be \$126 to \$663 billion dollars). Given that the benefits of regulations consistently exceed the costs, the need for any legislation that would make the issuance of regulations more difficult or time consuming is certainly in question.

In evaluating H.R. 10 (and debating whether additional restraints on the agencies are necessary or desirable), it is important to understand the many existing constraints (or checks) on federal agencies in developing and issuing regulations. First (and critically important), federal agencies are not free agents; they can only do what Congress has authorized them to do. Stated another way, federal regulatory agencies are not at liberty to do whatever they think might be a good idea – they can only issue regulations that implement existing law -- that is, laws that are duly enacted (passed by both Houses of Congress and signed by the President).

In addition, the process (as opposed to the substance) of rulemaking is already subject to several prescriptive federal statutes. The Administrative Procedure Act (APA), 5 U.S.C. 551 et seq., generally requires that agencies give notice of what they intend to do, along with their supporting data and analysis; that there be a meaningful opportunity for those affected by the proposal to comment (and to critique the data/methodology/details of the proposal/estimates of anticipated benefits and costs, etc.); and that the agencies respond to significant comments, explaining whether (and why) they agree or disagree with the comments received. Further, in the mid-1990's, Congress enacted the Unfunded Mandates Reform Act, 2 U.S.C. 1501 et seq., and it amended the Regulatory Flexibility Act with the Small Business Regulatory Enforcement Fairness Act, 5 U.S.C. 601, et seq., to name only two of several such statutes that require agencies to consult with entities that might be affected by proposed regulations and to do specific analyses regarding the impact of their proposals on those entities.

Regulatory agencies in the executive branch are also subject to Executive Order 12866, 58 Fed.Reg. 51735 (1993), which provides procedural and decisional criteria for developing major regulations. Among other things, agencies are to specify the legal authority under which they are proceeding, the problem(s) they are seeking to rectify, the estimated benefits and costs (both quantifiable and those that cannot be quantified), any less burdensome or costly alternatives to achieving the objectives, and ensure that the benefits of the proposal(s) justify the costs or explain why that cannot be achieved. E.O. 12866 and its salient principles, including centralized regulatory review, were explicitly reaffirmed by President Obama last week. The office that conducts the review of draft proposed and final regulations to ensure that they are consistent with the President's policies and preferences and the principles of E.O. 12866 is OIRA, which not only conducts its own review but also presides over an inter-agency process so that the input and perspectives of other federal agencies (often with conflicting mandates) can be taken into account. Similarly, interested or affected non-governmental entities can meet with officials at OIRA to present their views to an adviser to the President, who is ultimately the one accountable to the electorate for the actions of the federal regulatory agencies.

After the agencies have completed their work on a regulation (and there is final agency action within the meaning of the APA), the Congressional Review Act, another statute that originated with the Contract with America, kicks in. If the agency has gone beyond what Congress intended and there is agreement (simple majority vote) in both Houses of Congress (with expedited procedures in the Senate) and the concurrence of the President, that rule will be disapproved and be of no effect. A number of commentators have argued that the CRA has not been as effective as its proponents had hoped, and the findings in H.R. 3765 recited the fact that it "has only been exercised by Congress once since its enactment in 1996 to reject a rule." The number of disapprovals may not be indicative of the effect of the Act (especially because the original concept was to catch only the most egregious overreaching). At the same time, I do not doubt that its effectiveness could be enhanced by, for example, limiting its scope to major rules (from 50-100 a year) as opposed to the Congress' being inundated by all rules (several thousand a year), and/or by limiting the distribution of copies of each rule to only one committee of jurisdiction in each House rather than all committees of jurisdiction, so that attention could more easily be focused on the rules that warrant such attention.

Federal regulatory agencies are also subject to check by the courts. I need not belabor this point before this Committee, but any *ultra vires* action would not withstand judicial challenge, nor would any rule that is procedurally defective or substantively unsupported. We are a very litigious nation, and experience shows that those affected by new regulations are not the least bit reticent to seek judicial relief from what they perceive to be onerous rules issued by federal agencies. Indeed, virtually all controversial rules are challenged in court because there is little downside risk to mounting such an effort and hope seems to spring eternal even in the face of a robust supportive record.

While many major rules are controversial, there are other important rules that are not but that nonetheless would be captured by H.R. 10. Perhaps the best example of noncontroversial rules which are actually eagerly awaited each year by the regulated entities are those issued by the Department of Interior setting an annual quota for migratory bird hunting under the Migratory Bird Treaty; absent an implementing rule, no one could shoot game birds as they fly to or from Canada. Having been identified as a favored activity during the debate on the CRA, rules that affect a "regulatory program for commercial, recreational, or subsistence activity related to hunting, fishing, or camping" achieved the unique status of being exempt from many of the federal statutes enacted in the 1990s, and the drafters of H.R.10 have in like fashion carved out an exception specifically for these rules.

Although "hunting, fishing, or camping" rules are exempt from H.R. 10 (as are rules relating to monetary policy), many other types of rules favored by regulated entities are not exempt. It may be counter-intuitive to some, but it is not unusual for regulated entities to support or even champion certain rules – such as those that provide needed guidance or provide certainty or regularity for operations for the foreseeable future. For example, the automobile companies supported the Environmental Protection Agency (EPA)/Department of Transportation (DOT) joint rules for "Passenger Car and Light Truck Corporate Average Fuel Economy Standards for MY 2012-2016;" industry stakeholders supported the Department of Labor rule updating the Occupational Health and Safety Administration's "Cranes and Derricks" rule; the same for the Department of Energy's rule on "Weatherization Assistance for Program for Low Income Persons," which, among other things, reduced procedural burdens on evaluating certain housing applications.

There are also rules that specify the structure or eligibility for government programs, such as the Department of Education's rule on "Investing in Innovation Fund," and the Department of Defense (DOD) rule relating to the "Homeowners Assistance Program;" these rules enable the programs authorized and funded by Congress to begin to operate as they were envisioned or modified by Congress, and they are often eagerly awaited by the potential participants in the program. In a similar vein, there are multiple so-called transfer rules (which primarily cause transfers from taxpayers to program beneficiaries as specified by Congress), such as the Department of Agriculture's rules on the "Sugar Program," the "Emergency Loss Assistance and Livestock Forage Disaster Programs," and the "Biomass Crop Assistance Program," as well as the Department of Veterans Affairs' rule on the "Post 9/11 GI Bill." Delay in issuing the rules means delay in starting up or carrying on the programs.

Regulated entities may have been less enthusiastic about other rules issued during the Obama Administration, but the hands of the regulatory agencies are sometimes tied by the authorizing legislation. Examples of recent instances where the agency has scrupulously followed the provisions of the authorizing act – virtually no discretion was provided for, or exercised by, the agency -- include the DOT rule on "Positive Train Control," and the DOD rule on "Retroactive Stop Loss Special Pay Compensation." These rules simply carried out the law as passed by Congress, but if H.R. 10 is enacted, similar rules in the future would still need to be approved by both House of Congress and the President before they become effective.

Another category of rules worth considering are those that are important to public health and safety, which may be controversial with some, but highly desired by the vast majority. Examples include the Food and Drug Administration's "Shell Egg" rule dealing with salmonella; the DOT rules on "Reduced Stopping Distances for Truck Tractors" and "Standards for Increasing the Maximum Allowable Operating Pressure for Gas Transmission Pipelines;" and, in terms of equities, the Department of Justice (DOJ) rules on non-discrimination on the basis of disabilities.

In addition, in the foreseeable future, it is likely that several agencies would review exiting rules (the retrospective look-back called for by President

Obama last week) and propose to eliminate currently effective major rules; their attempt to do so, which would clearly be supported by the regulated entities, would nonetheless get caught in the H.R. 10 net, along with any deregulatory rules issued by this or a subsequent administration. (See Motor Vehicle Manufacturer Assn. v State Farm Mutual Automobile Insurance Co., 463 U.S. 29 (1983))

The proponents of H.R. 10 may argue that those rules that are acceptable (accordingly to a majority of then-current Members of Congress) will be approved, and only the objectionable ones will be stopped. Consider that the total number of major rules issued in CY 2010 was 94. Assuming that the Senate does not use its constitutional right (acknowledged in H.R. 10) to change the rules relating to the procedures of the Senate, and that the full time authorized in the bill -- for debate in the Senate on all debatable motions and appeals, the single quorum call, and the vote on the joint resolution itself (easily over four hours) --will be used for each rule considered, it is inconceivable that the Senate, with its other constitutional responsibilities (such as consideration of presidential nominations, work on appropriations bills from the House, etc.), could possibly find 90 blocks of time, or 50 or 25 or even 10 blocks of time sufficient for this process. Experience during the 111th Congress compels the conclusion that there will not be time to consider and approve even the most worthy rules. The "cost" to the economy and to society as a whole in terms of delay, uncertainty, and actual harm as a result of highly beneficial rules being held up or abandoned could be substantial, whereas the marginal "benefit" of having another significant procedural step before a major rule becomes effective -- as opposed to relying on the CRA process for a joint resolution of disapproval -- is likely to be minuscule.

Finally, but importantly, if most or even some final major regulations issued by federal agencies are barred from taking effect because one or both Houses of Congress do not – because of time constraints or philosophical or practical objections – explicitly approve the issuance of the regulations, then this bill would change dramatically the constitutional structure of our government. At the beginning of the 112th Congress, Members of this Chamber read aloud the Constitution, which assigns various responsibilities to the different branches of the federal government. The drafters of H.R.10 cite Section 1 of Article 1, which grants all legislative powers to the Congress. But equally important is Section 1 of Article II, which grants the executive power to the President. While the legislative branch is to make the laws, the executive branch is to "take care that the laws be faithfully executed."

Constitutional objections to this bill can be cast in at least two ways. First, assume that the Senate passes a joint resolution under H.R. 10 approving a major rule from a federal agency. The bill then goes to the House for a vote and the joint resolution is defeated. Can this easily be distinguished from INS v. Chadha, 462 U.S. 919 (1983), where the Supreme Court held that a determination by the Attorney General to suspend deportation that was disapproved by a one-House veto was unconstitutional, notwithstanding that the act authorizing the Attorney General's determination had specifically reserved a one-House veto in the event either House of Congress disagreed with the Attorney General's determination? It may not be enough to say that H.R. 10 incorporates bi-cameral and presentment (the requirements for constitutionality in Chadha) because in the case described above, one House alone would stop final agency action from becoming effective. Conceivably the supporters of H.R. 10 would argue that the agency action is not final (that is, the rule has no force or effect) because the intent and effect of H.R. 10 is to amend the underlying delegation of rulemaking authority to require explicit approval of any major rules by the Congress and the President. If this is their argument, then truth in legislating would call for being very clear – that these few pages of text in H.R. 10 are amending literally hundreds, in not thousands, of duly enacted laws – however long they have been on the books (i.e., for days or decades) – that delegated rulemaking authority (whether permitting or directing rulemakings) of every kind (eligibility criteria, standard setting, reporting requirements, articulation of enforcement policy) to every regulatory agency (executive branch or independent regulatory commissions).

Such an assertion leads to a somewhat more nuanced argument that H.R. 10 on its face may run afoul of the separation of powers principles our founding fathers embodied in the Constitution. In Morrison v Olson, 487 U.S. 654 (1988), Chief Justice Rehnquist set forth several tests for evaluating a statutory scheme under the separation of powers doctrine. One is that a statute is suspect if it "involves an attempt by Congress to increase its own powers at the expense of the executive branch." Much of the discussion surrounding H.R. 10 suggests that that may be an apt characterization of the sponsors' intent. Another test is whether an act of Congress "impermissibly interferes with the President's exercise of his constitutionally appointed function," which clearly includes the obligation to "take care that the laws be faithfully executed." For over a century, the executive branch has taken care to faithfully execute the laws by, among other things, developing and issuing regulations implementing legislation. Justice Scalia, who of all the Justices most aggressively guards the President's authority, relied in both Morrison v Olson and in Mistretta v. United States, 488 US 361 (1989), on the fact that the activities at issue in those cases were ones in which the executive had traditionally engaged. That characterization is clearly applicable here as well.

It is beyond dispute that if Congress were to require that the initiation of any prosecution by a U.S. Attorney or the Department of Justice would have to be approved by Congress before the prosecution could begin, such an act would be inconsistent with separation of powers. Does the same analysis hold for an act requiring prior approval of major regulations implementing duly enacted laws? Would such a requirement be viewed as an attempt by one branch to aggrandize itself at the expense of another? Would it be viewed as an attempt by one branch to impermissibly interfere with the ability of another branch to carry out its constitutional powers? Would it be viewed as an action that, again quoting from Morrison v. Olson, "unduly trammels on executive authority"? These questions, I believe, are not easily answered, nor are the concerns easily dismissed.

Thank you again for the opportunity to testify today. I look forward to answering any questions you may have.

INDEX

A

B

C

D

E

H

I

J

K

L

M

N

O

P

Q

R

S

W

Y